Wide Awakes, Invincibles, & Smokestackers

Early Baseball in Tall Timber Country
1869 - 1905

by Dave Larson

To Karen, with best wishes,
Dave Larson

Kirk House Publishers
Minneapolis, Minnesota

Wide Awakes, Invincibles, & Smokestackers
Early Baseball in Tall Timber Country, 1869-1905
by Dave Larson

Spellings in this book follow spellings of the historical documents quoted. For example: base ball, base-ball, and baseball reflect the evolution of the spelling.

Cover art and illustrations by Gary Daum.

Publisher's Cataloging-In-Publication Data
(Prepared by The Donohue Group, Inc.)

Larson, David M.
  Wide Awakes, Invincibles, & Smokestackers : early baseball in tall timber country, 1869-1905 /
by Dave Larson.
   p. : ill. ; cm.
  ISBN-13: 978-1-886513-45-7
  ISBN-10: 1-886513-45-7
1. Minor league baseball—Northwest, Pacific—History—19th century. 2. Minor league
baseball—Northwest, Pacific—History—20th century. 3. Baseball teams—Northwest, Pacific—
History—19th century. 4. Baseball teams—Northwest, Pacific—History—20th century. I. Title.
II. Title: Wide Awakes, Invincibles and Smokestackers

GV863.P33 L37 2006
796.357/64/0979

Library of Congress Control Number 20066925642

Kirk House Publishers, PO Box 390759, Minneapolis, MN 55439
Manufactured in the United States of America

All Busy—At the Game

Spent an
Hour
Trying to get a hearing
With prominent business men,
Each one disappearing
Before
I could even start to
Unwind
My
Line of
Talk.
Each one singing the same old tune,
"Busy engagements this afternoon."
Gave up!
Decided
I'd kill time
Until time
For my train by taking in the Ball game;
I arrived;
    Rich man,
        Poor man,
           Beggar man,
              Thief,
                Broker,
                  Banker,
                    Merchant, Chief!

Yes,
They were all there,
Every
Blasted
One of them.
Every busy Minnie
Who
Hadn't
Time
To talk
Business.
Shouting,
"Soak 'em!"
"Kill the umpire!"
"Robber!"
"Slide!"
Each one yelling like a loon,
Busy men that afternoon!

No. 16   May 13th 1891

This is to Certify that

Mr. E L Colyer

Is the owner of ten shares of the Cap-
ital Stock of the Bellingham Bay Baseball
Association, and is entitled to admission for
Self and lady for the season
of 1891

Paul Dormitzer

Secretary

NOT TRANSFERABLE

Contents

* The name of the game was spelled differently at various times in the history of the game (base ball, base-ball, and baseball). The spellings in this book reflects the usage of the time.

Introduction

DAVID DILGARD, HISTORIAN, EVERETT, WASHINGTON, PUBLIC LIBRARY

Somebody once said that life is what happens while you're making other plans. Sometimes history and the writing of it emerge likewise, that is to say, when you're looking for something else. Dave Larson was putting the finishing touches on a thorough historical examination of Everett's Bethania College when he was distracted by a mere detail, a little footnote that eventually transformed itself into the present book.

It turns out that a century ago one of the teachers at Bethania was the wife of a man named Walter Thornton, who at first glance appeared to be some sort of underemployed derelict. Upon closer inspection Walter was revealed to be Snohomish County's first Major League baseball player.

For a fellow like Dave, that tidbit was irresistibly tempting, and before long the stray footnote was blossoming into the garland of wonderful episodes enclosed herein, portraits of a primordial pastime drawn from accounts vividly reported by pioneer Northwest sports writers. These pieces have been preserved and presented here largely verbatim, with much of their integrity as journalistic artifacts intact.

These ancient innings provide an amazing lens through which to view the lives and attitudes of previous generations, especially when we see it through the eyes of gifted and occasionally inspired journalists. And while it was indubitably a "National Pastime," baseball has always been a site-specific activity exhibiting all the idiosyncrasies of place. It speaks graphically of the people and places of a lost era while compelling us, as the best history always does, to perceive and compare the contemporaneous correspondences with the here and now.

Sometimes history has the feel of those yellowed formal portraits, where stiff and expressionless subjects rigidly await the camera's judgement. Larson gives us the historiographical antithesis-revealing candid snapshots of our unsuspecting ancestors at play, glimpses that evoke their personalities and pursuits in ways that inform our perceptions of the past in important ways.

Unexpected pleasures await you. Herein you will find the story of the regional roots of the great American sport, from the dawn of "Base Ball Fever" in the 1870s through that triumphal 1905 season of Everett's intrepid "Smokestackers," told almost entirely in the words of the original scribes who witnessed and recorded it. It has been assembled for your edification and delight by a researcher whose eye for detail and thoroughness of scholarship are exceeded only by his profound affection for the subject at hand.

Dedication and Foreword

"Most of the early sports columnists were humorists, and much latitude was permitted them in the name of entertainment. They needed it, for the columnist's relentless obligation is to find something worth writing about when the news is dull."

NICHOLAS DAWIDOFF in *The Catcher Was a Spy.*

This book is dedicated to the early sportswriters of the Pacific Northwest, and with special thanks to those perceptive scribes who recognized the importance of baseball in the social life of the whole community, and who reported it in a wonderfully entertaining style.

From the late 1800's until well into the 1900's baseball was indisputably the National Game. This status was reflected in the newspaper coverage given the game; baseball was sometimes the only news reported on the front page.

In Territorial days small town newspapers were usually weeklies, and the owner, publisher, editor and sportswriter were often the same person. Some of the newspapermen were directly involved with their local baseball team. C.L. Clemans, co-owner of the *Snohomish* (Washington) *Tribune* in the 1890's, had been a star athlete at Stanford University; for several years he played as a regular on the Snohomish team. James Powers, editor of the *Bellingham Bay Mail*, was the umpire of the 1875 game played at Bellingham Bay. Clayton Packard, editor of the *Snohomish Eye*, is identified as the umpire on the 1883 Snohomish Pacifics team picture. With the editor as umpire, there was no carping in the newspapers about the officiating.

In order to sell newspapers as well as to vent their personal pique, those early journalistic crusaders flailed away at everything that bumped up against their biases including editors of neighboring newspapers, politicians in general, and umpires in particular who with diabolical intent caused the defeat of their hometown heroes. There were risks involved in this lurid journalism. In July, 1883, Isaac Cathcart, Snohomish pioneer saloon and hotel man, was tried in Territorial Court on a charge of assault upon Clayton Packard of the *Snohomish Eye*, but was acquitted at a jury trial.

The most outrageous editor was James W. Connella of the *Everett News*. The *History of Snohomish County* (1926, Wm. Whitfield, editor) relates that in 1893 "the aggressive and spiteful Connella got into serious difficulties with Colonel Vernon, editor of the *Everett Times*, who twice had Connella arrested on charges of criminal libel, but the vituperative editor was acquitted each time... Every month of its existence under the fiery guidance of Connella, who was a cripple, was a stormy one. It all culminated in October, 1898, when the ill-tempered editor shot and killed Ole Nelson, a well-known and popular wood dealer" who Connella accused of lying about him. Connella was arrested and charged with murder. Public sentiment was strongly against Connella, so his trial was moved across Puget Sound to Kitsap County where a jury acquitted him on the grounds that because he was a cripple he most certainly must have fired in self defense. Fearing violence from Nelson's friends in Everett, Connella left the area never to return. Several of the articles in this book are from Connella's tenure at the *Everett News*.

Virtually all the information about early baseball has been gleaned from old newpapers. Unfortunately many newspaper collections are not complete, so there are gaps in the history that can never by filled. Enough has survived, however, to give a look both at the game and the social context in which it was played in the pioneer days of the Pacific Northwest.

DAVE LARSON

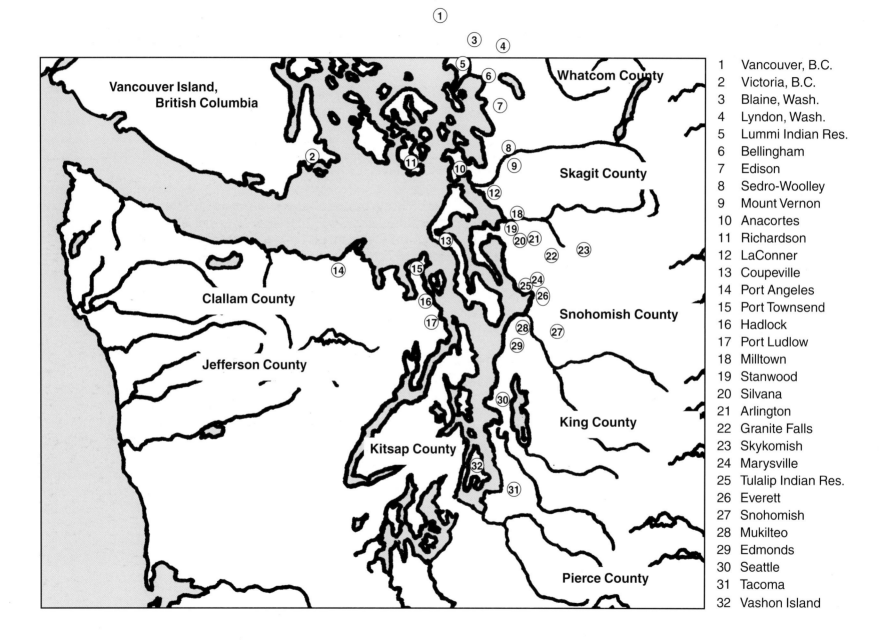

① Vancouver, B.C.

③ ④

⑤

⑥ Whatcom County

Vancouver Island,
British Columbia

⑦

② ⑧

⑪ ⑨ Skagit County

⑩

⑫

⑱

⑲

⑬ ⑳ ㉑

⑭ ㉒ ㉓

⑮ ㉔

Clallam County ㉕

⑯ ㉖

⑰ Snohomish County

㉘ ㉗

㉙

Jefferson County

King County

Kitsap County

㉚

㉜

㉛

Pierce County

1 Vancouver, B.C.
2 Victoria, B.C.
3 Blaine, Wash.
4 Lyndon, Wash.
5 Lummi Indian Res.
6 Bellingham
7 Edison
8 Sedro-Woolley
9 Mount Vernon
10 Anacortes
11 Richardson
12 LaConner
13 Coupeville
14 Port Angeles
15 Port Townsend
16 Hadlock
17 Port Ludlow
18 Milltown
19 Stanwood
20 Silvana
21 Arlington
22 Granite Falls
23 Skykomish
24 Marysville
25 Tulalip Indian Res.
26 Everett
27 Snohomish
28 Mukilteo
29 Edmonds
30 Seattle
31 Tacoma
32 Vashon Island

Chapter One: Base Ball Games, 1869-1899

Base Ball

The *bon ton* of Port Townsend, are organizing a base ball club. They have been in practive about two months, and we understand from a very good authority that they intend to send a challenge to the San Francisco B.B.C. and pay their expenses to play the game at this place.

Base Ball

On Saturday last the Red Rover B. B. Club challenged the old Union B. B. Club to play a game of base ball; the challenege was accepted. The Red Rovers are:

Loren B. Hastings, Jr.	Captain; catcher
Alfred A. Plummer, Jr.	Right field
L.T. Seavey	Pitcher
Nelson Lauback	1st base
Isaac Calhoun	2nd base
Daniel Hill	3rd base
George Trenholm	Left field
Cyrus Britt	Center Field
Frank Clinger	Short stop

The Union Club comprised several gentlemen of the town. The score of the Red Rovers at the close of the game was fifty-nine runs, against sixty-eight by the Union. The play of the Red Rovers was generally good, their fielding especially. It was only in the batting that the Unions beat them. Pull up, boys; you made the big 'uns *sore*, even if you didn't beat them—there's some gratification in that.

NOTE: *Not enough issues of these papers have survived to permit a follow-up on these stories.*

The First Base Ball Game Played in Whatcom County, Washington Territory

The earliest Base Ball game in Whatcom County was contested on a sand spit in Bellingham Bayon the first of May, 1875. As recounted in the newspaper:

"Several clerks, a mining engineer and two trappers formed a ball team which was called the 'Wide Awakes,' and challenged the coal miners in the Black Diamond Mine, who were operating in the side of Sehome Hill, to a game of base ball.

"Now, few of the miners had ever seen a base ball and most of them scarcely knew the game existed, but they were not about to take a back seat for mere clerks, engineers and trappers, so they accepted the challenge. John Jenkins was then a miner in the Black Diamond Mine and was chosen to head the team. He knew a few of the points of the game, and upon him fell the task of divulging them to his teammates. There was only one base ball in the town at the time, and as this was in the possession of the Wide Awakes, all the Black Diamonds could do was to sit and wait for the day set apart for the game.

"Base ball being more of a curiosity than a craze in the town at that time, the coal mine and the little sawmill were shut down for the day so that everybody might witness the contest. The miners had picked out the nine largest men in their midst to win the honors of the day for them, and when they strutted on the spit, they were a formidable-looking aggregation. The Wide Awakes were already on hand and the game was soon started, with James Powers, editor of the *Bellingham Bay Mail*, as umpire.

"The Wide Awakes won the toss and chose the field. The first miner to bat was the largest man on the team, and the Wide Awake pitcher threw him two straight strikes. The third ball delivered struck the ground and came bouncing over the plate. This looked good to the big man, so taking his bat like a golf stick, he swung on the sphere. It shot along the ground with the speed of a cannon ball, and the Wide Awake slab artist, not daring to risk his fingers, stopped the horsehide with his feet and tossed it to the man covering the first sack. 'Out!' cried Umpire Powers, and then the miners protested. They declared that the pitcher had no right to stop the ball with his feet, saying that base ball should only be played with the hands. After several minutes of dispute they were finally convinced that the play was legal and the game proceeded.

"Robert Ramsey of the Black Diamonds was the second man to bat. The first thing he did was to hit a pop-up fly. Catcher Charley Donovan got under the ball ready to catch it, but as it came down Ramsey hit it another crack and ran to first base. Another argument started, and so on through the game. After nearly every play a lengthy dispute followed. After several hours of playing the Wide Awakes were adjudged the winners, but the score is still unknown. Postmaster Hugh Eldridge said it would have taken an expert accountant to have kept track of the points made by the Wide Awakes."

The teams were composed as follows:

WIDE AWAKES		BLACK DIAMONDS
Osborn	Pitcher	Woods, Captain
Donovan, Captain	Catcher	Wright
Engle	First base	Jenkins
Steinway	Second base	Hayes
Webster	Third base	Saunders
Wood	Shortstop	Morris
Jones	Right field	Ramsey
Upson	Center field	Webber
Mann	Left field	Thomas

(In early pioneer days in the Pacific Northwest cleared flat areas big enough for a ball field were mostly on river bottom-lands and sand spits, and there they could only play until the tide came in.)

The First Published Report of Base Ball in Snohomish County, Washington Territory

The earliest newspaper in Snohomish County was *The Northern Star,* first published in January, 1876 and issued weekly until May, 1879. The Star's first mention of Base Ball was in August, 1877:

"The Base Ball epidemic is increasing. Several foolish attempts have been made to catch the ball in the mouth...

"Base Ball fever is increasing in violence...

"No fatal case of Base Ball yet. One member discovered several new planets by attempting to catch a sky flyer on the top of his head, and another, failing to jump high enough to catch the ball in his mouth, took it in the eye, and saw clusters of stars not marked in the geography of the heavens, besides several new comets. Still another drove some of his digits up to his wrist, and another ornaments his dexter mauler with several linen handkerchiefs. The undertaker is waiting impatiently...

"A match game was played between Snohomish City and the Lowell Base Ball Clubs. Both these clubs are foundlings we suppose, for they are both unnamed. We suggest The Orphans...

"The Snohomish Base Ball Club ought to be christened The Charitables; they were magnanimous enough to allow the Lowell Club to beat them two to one."

1877 was also the year of the first organized Base Ball Club in Seattle, the Alkis.

WASHINGTON STANDARD • OLYMPIA, WASHINGTON TERRITORY • AUGUST 1879

The Blue Jays of Snohomish City

Interestingly—surprisingly—one of the first base ball clubs in Snohomish County was a women's team! In August of 1879 the *Washington Standard* newspaper published in Olympia, Washington Territory, reported:

"The young ladies of Snohomish have organized a base ball club. They stand ready to play any of the clubs on the Sound...

"The boys of the Olympia base ball club are anxious to test the agility of the young ladies of Snohomish."

Then in September, 1879, the Washington Standard reported:

"The 'Blue Jays' is the name of the young ladies base ball club at Snohomish City...

"It is said that the 'Blue Jay' Base Ball Club, of Snohomish City, composed of young ladies, have adapted their mode of playing to feminine peculiarities. F'rinstance, the pitcher stands with back to the batter and throws the ball over her shoulder; the catcher captures the ball with her apron, and the runner announces her arrival at each base by a shrill shriek. They play at the Territorial Fair, and we predict they will draw a bigger crowd than a circus."

Unfortunately, the game at the Territorial Fair was rained out.

The Blue Jays were organized during an interval when there was no newspaper in Snohomish City, so there was no local coverage of their base ball games.

One player took the ball in the eye and saw clusters of stars.

The Baseball Boys at Seattle

In September, 1883, Seattle put on an extravagant welcome celebration for Henry Villard, head of the Northern Pacific Railroad, hoping to extract from him a commitment to connect Seattle to the transcontinental rail system. Among the events were two baseball games between the Seattle Reds and the Snohomish Pacifics. Games were contested at the Seattle Driving Park Association grounds which were reached by train from Seattle.

Last Wednesday, about 9 or 10 A.M., some several dames and damsels, gallant swains, elegant dudes, horny-handed grangers and Pacific B.B.C.'s took passage on board the steamer *Daisy* bound for the "Queen City of the West." Thursday we could not play; Friday, ditto, as the "second coming" — of Villard, I mean—was momentarily expected.

Saturday the S.D.P.A. gave the Pacific B.B.C. a benefit game from which they netted the enormous (?) sum of $16. Only five innings were played, owing to the late commencement of the game. The Pacifics won, 6 to 3.

In the hurry-scurry of getting aboard the train for home, one of our heavy-weights, who had ventured to take his girl to the show, forgot all about the fair damsel, and struck for home, leaving his charmer to the tender mercies of a frowning world. When about half way to Seattle one of the boys inquired: "Chip, where's your girl?" Then and there was enacted one of the saddest scenes it has ever been our misfortune to behold. The heavy-weight stood for a moment as if paralyzed; then the deep fountains of his gushing soul busted her boiler, and manly tears in torrents rushed, bubbled and splashed that ancient flat-car o'er. Strong men grasped the frantic youth and gently sat him down; placed him in a cosy, quiet corner, and tenderly piled old boots, railroad iron and Renton coal upon his bruised and bleeding form. Alas, nothing could still the panting, bleeding heart; he sobbed and moaned, but still the iron horse carried him farther from her. Remorselessly and with maniacal screeches it left in the dim distance his love, his hope, his chick-a-bid-da-be.

THE SEATTLE POST-INTELLIGENCER • 1883

The Match Game

SEPTEMBER 18: On Sunday the much talked of match between the Snohomish and Seattle base ballists took place on the Driving Park Association grounds. The Snohomish boys did fine fielding while that done by the Seattle team was bungling. On the second inning the score stood Snohomish 7, Seattle 1. At this juncture the metropolitan boys braced up a little, and at the close of the fifth inning, when the game ceased, the score stood 14 for Snohomish and 8 for Seattle. The Snohomish club was declared champion and was awarded the $100 Association prize.

To Base Ballists

OCTOBER 6: The Snohomish base ball boys crow most vigorously over their defeat of the Seattle boys, and are pretty loud in telling about it. Well, they are entitled to crow, and we hope they will crow on until they infuse into the boys here a little more spirit. The spirit to overcome all obstacles and determine to win. From being called champions the Seattle boys have gone down, down, down, until they stand so low in the scale of players that the meanest club that can be got together no longer hesitates to dare them, and on trial, beats them. For shame, boys! You have the most material outside of Portland to draw from, and presumably the best. That you should through sloth allow yourself to be so disgracefully, so repeatedly and so ignominiously beaten, and then be so taunted and insulted over it, is humiliating and painful to all in town. Either disband your organization or get yourselves in trim to face with fair prospects of success any club on the coast.

One of the Snohomish players forgot all about his girl.

Standing, L to R: *John Delfel; W.R. Booth; Clayton Packard, Umpire; Oliver Dunstan; C.A. Missimer, Scorer; Homer Moore.* ***Sitting, L to R:*** *H.F. Jackson, Manager; Archie Anderson; R.O. Welts; J. Van Bowen; J.W. Fobes.*

SEPTEMBER 19: Immediately after the game Sunday it was announced from the Grand Stand that "Seattle challenges Snohomish to play a match game of base ball, within thirty days, for $500. When, however, the matter came to be sifted down, it stood about thus: "We, Seattle, will play the United States of America against Snohomish." The Pacifics offered to name twelve men, with Seattle to do likewise. But, of course, this would not serve their purpose. They only wanted to make a bluff, and enjoy the exquisite felicity of listening to their own glib and flexible tongues.

SEPTEMBER 26: The Pacifics have accepted the challenge of the Seattle club to play for the purse of $500 a side, and on Friday last deposited a forfeit of $100. If the ex-champions do not "take water" the game will take place at Snohomish City on Saturday, October 6, 1883. It is understood, however, that Seattle is not to import any professionals, and the Pacifics are to play only members of their club. This will be the most important game ever played north of San Francisco, and many admirers of the national game are coming from a distance to witness it. Boys, give them the best that you have in the box, and we have no doubt but you will continue to hold the championship of the Territory.

OCTOBER 3: Since the above was put in type the Seattle club has "flunked." The $100 forfeit, that the Pacifics sent to Seattle to cover a like amount supposed to have been put up by the Seattle club, was returned on Friday last. In first challenging the Pacifics, then doing a superfluous amount of heavy "blowing," and finally, when they saw the Pacifics meant business, crawling into their holes, they have shown their asinine propensities, and ought to feel pretty cheap over the result.

Judging from the reception of the Pacifics two weeks ago, they do not know how to treat a visiting club civilly, and before again entering the diamond it would be a pious idea for them to study a little base ball etiquette.

The Squire block was cut down several feet, leaving an abrupt bank

Snohomish to the Front

The match game of base ball at Snohomish last Saturday, between the Seattle Reds and the Pacifics of Snohomish, resulted in a victory for the latter by a score of 21 to 11.

The Seattle boys were most hospitably entertained by their Snohomish brethren. After the game they were banqueted, and later in the evening a ball was given in their honor in Cathcart's beautiful hall. Arrangements are already making for a return game in this city.

Some person wanted to know how it was that the Seattle boys were beaten, when a knowing one replied: "They were beaten because they were outplayed. The Snohomish club is in thorough practice, while the members of the Seattle club have never played together but once or twice, and a practice game is something entirely unknown to them." The fact is, there are no grounds in Seattle on which the boys can practice with any degree of satisfaction. The Squire block in North Seattle was pretty fair before the streets surrounding it were graded and cut down several feet, thus leaving an abrupt bank on two sides of the block. However, the recent defeat will not result disastrously, as the boys are already discussing the propriety and advisability of playing a series of practice games before accepting another challenge.

PACIFICS vs REDS

The Umpire the Strongest Player of the Seattle Club

Last Friday noon the steamer *Nellie* with about thirty excursionists, including several members of the Pacifics base ball club, left Snohomish for Seattle, where the second game of the series was to be played on Saturday with the Seattle Reds. The steamer *Josephine* followed early Saturday morning with the remainder of the club and a few excursionists, but unfortunately ran upon a sand bar at the mouth of the river at high (!) tide, and part of the base ballists were obliged to row to Mukilteo, a distance of seven miles, in an open boat, while the remainder footed it around the beach. Here they remained until the steamer *Washington* came along from Whatcom. When the boys arrived at the ball grounds about four o'clock they were pretty badly broken up, so to speak.

The game was delayed by a long palaver over the selection of an umpire. Malarkey, a Portland base ballist, was finally agreed upon, and the game was called at 4:30. After the first inning the glaringly unfair decisions of the umpire showed that it was the intention to defeat the Pacifics at all hazards. At the commencement of the sixth inning the score stood 4 to 13 in favor of the Reds, and our boys were about ready to throw up the sponge. The phenomenal playing of our gallant center fielder, however, encouraged them to play it out, and at the close of the game they were but four scores behind, 15 to 19. The pitching of Fairbairn of the Reds, the "holy terror" who was so badly feared, did not paralyze our boys to any great extent, and he was hit about as often as were Welts or Van Bowen of the Pacifics. The reception of the Pacifics at Seattle was not quite so cordial as was that of the Reds at Snohomish, but expecting nothing more, the Pacifics were not disappointed. However, all our boys ask in the remaining games is a "square deal." Shortly after the game two of the Pacifics were informed by a reliable gentleman that Malarkey, the umpire, had $75 staked on the game. This accounts for many things.

The Baseballists were obliged to row to Mukilteo

The Championship Settled

Details of the Base Ball Game Played Saturday Between the Seattle Reds and the Pacifics of Snohomish.

A party of fifteen Seattleites, including the playing nine of the Seattle Base Ball Club, left on the *Nellie* for Snohomish City at 6 o'clock Saturday morning to participate in and witness the third game of the series between the above mentioned club and the Pacifics of the visited city. The first contest occured at Snohomish on May 31st, when the Reds were defeated by a score of 21 to 11. The second came off at the grounds of the Seattle club, and the home nine scored a creditable victory, 19 to 15. Saturday's game was the deciding contest, and its result must be accepted by all interested as settling decisively the question as to who are the Territorial champions for the season of 1884.

Arriving at Snohomish at about 1 in the afternoon, the Reds quickly donned their uniforms and repaired to the field. Time was called shortly after 2 o'clock by Mr. Hinckley of Snohomish, who acted as umpire.

The Reds outplayed their opponents at every point, both fielding and batting; in the latter making a most noteworthy record, no man among them being put out on strikes, and all indulging in heavy hitting. Fielding features for the Reds were Kenney's superb support of Fairbairn's wonderfully effective pitching, he catching 10 out on strikes and one on a foul tip, and Fairbairn's taking in two red hot liners on the fly from the bat. There was little for the outfield to do because the Pacifics batted but two balls outside the diamond. On the part of the Pacifics, Booth on first, and Delfel in left field, did excellent service.

The ground was an ordinary meadow, hummocky and with ditches and stumps, a wretched place for effective playing by a visiting team. The genial Roll, the Red's short-stop "bobbed up serenely" from behind a big hummock whenever duty called, and got in his customary reliable playing.

The Reds did not play their half of the ninth inning, being already in the lead by 24 runs, 31 to 7. The game ended about 4:30.

THE SEATTLE REDS.

THE

SEATTLE BASE BALL CLUB,

Champions of the Pacific Northwest.

(Oregon, Washington Territory and British Columbia.)

Season of 1884.

1
E. W. Burnell,
Change Field.

2
J. V. Wyckoff,
2d. Base.

3
D. H. Blackmarr,
Cen. Field.

4
G. W. Roll,
Short Stop.

5
F. Coulter,
3d Base.

6
A. B. Ensign,
President and Manager.

7
J. T. Reddish,
Capt. and 1st Base.

8
W. R. Thornell,
Sec'y and Left Field.

9
G. E. Starrett,
Change Catcher.

10
W. J. Kenney,
Catcher.

11
J. E. Fairbairn,
Pitcher.

12
H. R. Jacobs,
Right Field and Change Pitcher.

That Base-ball Game

To the Editor:

Noting a piece in the Snohomish Eye concerning the game of base-ball played between the Clipper base-ball club, of Stanwood, and the Washington club, of Florence, on October 11 (won by Florence 46 to 4), I think it no more than right to set the facts before the public.

During the summer a party of young men at Stanwood organized a base-ball club, and as usual, parties up the river at Florence, always imitative, never in the lead, also organized. They made one grand mistake, however; they named their club Washington, after a man who never told a lie.

In a very short time thereafter the Washingtons challenged the Clippers of Stanwood. The Clippers went to Florence and played the game, beating them 16 to 12. The Clippers then challenged the Washingtons for a return game.

Then they were even more successful, beating their opponents by a score of 40 to 15. The Washingtons then challenged the Clippers to play for $10 a side.

As soon as the challenge was accepted by the Clippers, the Washingtons sent to Snohomish (and I think also to Philadelphia) for a pitcher and a catcher. When the Stanwood boys objected to having outsiders in the game, Florence swore with big and broad oaths that the imported pitcher and catcher were members of the Washingtons and had been at work near Florence all summer. Parties living near Florence warned the Clippers of the improved stock imported for their benefit, not wishing to have the stigma cast upon their town of imposing upon visitors.

It is always customary among gentlemanly base-ball players to treat the visiting club as well as possible, and not ask them to play on an empty stomach, which these Washingtons did.

We will now see what the Washingtons paid for the honor of beating the Clippers. They paid their pitcher $10; catcher, $10, besides paying their hirelings' expenses, which probably amounted

Continued on next page

to $20 more, making a total of $40 out-of-pocket, plus lost character, $60—all to beat the Clippers, when I can pick out nine old women anywhere in the the county that can beat the Washingtons.

Now about the challenges which there is so much blow about. Two fellows, who looked like tramps and also as though they never saw $100 in their lives, came to Stanwood and proposed we put up $50 forfeit on a game of base-ball between the Clippers and Washingtons for $100. Who could have been green enough to entrust $50 in their care? If these two were a specimen of the Washingtons, no wonder the visiting club at Florence went without their dinner, as I am certain these two representatives of the Washingtons did not have enough money in their pockets to pay for their dinner the day they were here. They even claimed the right to name who should play on the Stanwood nine.

Yours,
BASE-BALL

This Was a Corker

Seattle and Tacoma Play Twenty-two Innings

Ye gods! but the baseball enthusiasts went wild yesterday afternoon. Tooth and nail Tacoma and Seattle struggled for victory. From the twelfth to the twenty-second inning pandemonium swayed the crowd. Such cheering and shouting, such mad flaying of the benches with heavy soled boots and shoes, such demonical yells, and such rattling of clapboards on the grand stand with canes and umbrellas, in fact such a fury of discordant and ear-splitting noises, has seldom been heard at any time in any country. In proportion to the shouting and cheering assemblage, the crowd that egged both teams on to victory at the Tacoma baseball grounds yesterday afternoon could not be outdone even by a wildly excited throng witnessing a closely contested Roman chariot race.

Indeed, from the start interest in the game was intense, and as inning after inning rolled up the excitement was fanned beyond the white heat point and passed into thin air, and then the hilarity became infectious. Everybody yelled. Mutual friends jabbed each other in the ribs, smashed hats, stamped, roared, hurrahed, screamed themselves hoarse and fell back into their seats exhausted. Up to the fifteenth and sixteenth inning the fellows who don't indulge in "unseemly hilarity" at a baseball game kept comparatively straight faces, but as the astonishing record kept on discounting itself even the stoics yielded and began "whooping it up" with the majority.

Boys on the bleachers blew rasping sounds from big tin horns, and let out cat calls that brought swarms of people to the surrounding house tops and telegraph and telephone poles. Serenity went over to Mount Rainier and the crowd cheered and perspired. For once the "kickers" got the worth of their money. They admitted it and will hereafter attend all the games.

Both teams worked as if the result were a matter of life and death. Determination, grim and sullen, possessed them toward the finish. They did not laugh. Nothing seemed ridiculous to them. Fully one-eighth of the audience of 900 was from Seattle. They encouraged their laddies magnificently.

Several times was the phenomenal game lost and won. By the most careful, close playing Seattle tied, in the same inning, every chalk made by the home team, after the limit was reached in the ninth. (NOTE: The visiting team batted last.) The fielding was admirable, and the same must be said of the running of the bases. Powell's oft-repeated injunction while coaching his men, "Everybody play ball, close and careful," seemed to have gone home to both teams.

Of course after so much pounding, the ball became punky towards the end of the game, and the best the batter could hope to do was to send it out in the territory of the outfield. As a result many were the flies taken into camp.

Above all Donahue's pitching is deserving of the honors. He pitched the twenty-two innings without showing the least sign of losing his grip. Then in the twenty-second inning he hit safely and was advanced to third on a double. The Seattle second baseman muffed a fly ball and the undaunted Donahue scored what proved to be the winning run.

A Record Breaker

The Longest Purely Professional Game Ever Played

Yesterday's Seattle-Tacoma game of twenty-two innings was a record breaker, being the longest strictly professional game ever played. There is but one longer game on record, which was played at Boston, May 11, 1877, between the amateur Harvard college nine and Manchester, the score being 0 to 0 in twenty-four innings. Previous to yesterday the longest professional game on record was that played August 17, 1882, at Providence, between the Providence and Detroit teams, the score being 1 to 0 in eighteen innings. The game was won for Providence in the eighteenth inning by a home run hit by Charley "Old Hoss" Radbourne, the Providence pitcher.

Donahue established another record—that of pitching twenty-two consecutive innings under the overhand style of pitching rule. At the time of the famous twenty-four inning game between Harvard and Manchester, the underhand style of pitching, which was not nearly so great a strain as there is under the present rule, was in vogue.

The Game Bulletined

An Immense Crowd Watches the Game by Innings

The results of yesterday's wonderful game at Tacoma, which was bulletined by innings in front of the *Post-Intelligencer* office, drew a larger crowd than has often gathered to see the game itself at the Madison Street park. During the first part of the game the usual number watched the blackboard, but when the extra innings began to be chalked up the crowd started to grow in numbers and enthusiasm. By the twelfth inning fully 500 people had assembled and blockaded not only the sidewalk but the entire street, while the steps and landing of the *Post-Intelligencer* office were packed to their fullest capacity.

A description of every play was received over the wires and announced to the crowd, which waited with feverish expectancy for something new. The good plays of Tacoma, as well as of Seattle, received recognition, and as goose-egg after goose-egg was marked up, the intensity of the cheering grew. At two different times, when, in the fifteenth and eighteenth innings, Seattle promptly caught up after Tacoma had taken the lead by the seemingly winning run, the scene would have done credit to the most confirmed set of "fans" that ever graced the stands during a closely contested game. Staid business and professional men jostled against newsboys and vied with them in shouting themselves hoarse, forgetting all about the dinners that were waiting in vain for them. When in the twenty-second Tacoma scored what proved to be the winning run, it was generously applauded. The announcement that Seattle had failed to again tie the score brought an almost utter silence for a few seconds; then a burst of cheers followed in recognition of the magnificent performance of the two teams.

George E. MacDonald

George MacDonald was one of the long line of talented writers who spent some time in the West. He was born in Gardiner, Maine, on April 11th, 1857, trained as a printer's apprentice in New York City, then headed for California and newspaper work in 1887. He came North to Snohomish, Washington, in 1891 and accepted a position as co-editor of *The Eye* newspaper. MacDonald didn't know much about baseball when he arrived, but he was a keen observer of the scene and wrote wonderfully entertaining articles describing the context in which games were played. In one three column article, the first two columns gleefully reported a blow-by-blow account of a fight that took place before the game.

In November, 1893, MacDonald moved back to New York, leaving behind a legacy of well-crafted writing for us to enjoy. A Freethinker, he spent the rest of his career as the editor of the *Truth Seeker* publications in New York. He died July 21st, 1944.

The following articles published in *The Eye* newspaper in 1892 and 1893 were written by George MacDonald.

Descriptions of the Baseball Scene

Season of 1893

June 5: "The Snohomish first baseman's reach is immense and his hands of such ample capacity that he has only to put them up in the form of a hopper and the ball disappears in their depths like a swallow diving into a chimney."
(Everett 5, Snohomish 4)

July 31: "The Seattle Teamsters had on crimson uniforms that looked as though they had been dyed in the blood of victims slain upon the field of battle."
"The umpire was much admired not only for his beauty, which is of the southern type, but also for the firmness with which he maintained his decisions, especially the erroneous ones."
(Snohomish 9, Teamsters 3)

September 6: "Clemons had merely to put out his hands and the ball froze to them like drops of winter rain on an apple tree."
(Snohomish 8, Port Gamble 1)

September 18: "Zulu Bill Simmons, the Seattle Maroons' pitcher, is a whizzer. His face is swarthy and calculated to inspire terror. If he were throwing the assagai spear of his native Zululand instead of a leather sphere, he couldn't do it any more wickedly than he lets the ball go."
(Snohomish 10, Maroons 4)

October 12: "The umpire's decisions on balls were errors, on strikes they were crimes, on fouls they were outrages, and at the bases they were sins against the Holy Ghost."
(Port Gamble 9, Snohomish 4)

October 26: "The twilight gave the Knights temporary advantage, but the moon came up like a cold deck in a social game of poker."
(Odd Fellows 27, Knights of Pythias 23)

A Reporter's Journey to Tualco

The Day Was Hot, The Horse Was Stiff,
and The Rider A Tenderfoot

A game of ball was played yesterday between the Snohomish Cyclones and the Tualco Chinooks.

Early in the morning the reporter encountered a lot of the Snohomish boys with bats and chest protectors and masks, hurrying toward the wharf, and he insanely determined to follow on horseback. It was the reporter's chief concern to find an animal that was safe, because he had not been on a horse's back since the year 1870, when he bestrode a steed that drew the cultivator between rows of corn in Cheshire County, New Hampshire. The man who lets horses at the stable first brought out a big supple brute with a vicious eye. When the reporter inquired if the horse was safe, the man acknowledged that the animal had bucked several riders' teeth out and had thrown one of them so high that when he hit the ground it killed him. During this recital the horse eyed the reporter and sized him up, and when, as directed, the stable hand led the mankiller back to the stall, the four-legged rascal turned his head to cast a very contemptuous glare upon the writer.

When the would-be rider told the stable hand that he had not mounted a horse since 1870, and had never sat in a saddle, the stable hand, with the remark that a rocking horse might answer best, went away and led in a gray little nag, built like a cracker, and saddled him. This horse was warranted safe. The correspondent vaulted lightly to the saddle, having one man to hold the horse and another to boost the rider to his seat.

The trip began merrily, the reporter being fresh and the horse inclined to prance. The rider had a rose in his buttonhole and let one arm flop by his side after the approved style. When a carriage was caught and passed, a passenger observed that the reporter rode as though he were a part of the horse. He did not specify which part.

The writer noted an unusual phenomenon as he proceeded; namely, that he was a good deal hotter, a good deal sweatier, and rather unhappier than the horse that carried him. He also got thirstier. He drank water greedily, stopping wherever a spring came out beside the road. A man inquired, with a degree of sarcasm, how much the horseman would pay a boy to ride the horse back to Snohomish and let the reporter walk.

All the same, the rider stuck to his steed and tied up at a fence near the school house. The ball ground lies in a pasture to the west of the school; a high fence has been constructed for a back-stop.

The Snohomish athletes were on the ground and the Tualco nine, with four or five Indian members, strolled about and looked at the build of their adversaries. A week ago the Snohomish boys went sailing up the river to do up the natives, and came back done up. Yesterday they girded on their canvas shoes with spikes in them and hardened their hands by spatting them across hydrants, telegraph poles, and the smoke stack of the steamer as they went along, determined to win or die, or both.

Snohomish went first to bat and scored four runs before the side was out. They are better, possibly, in the field than at the bat. Walter Thornton sailed the ball down the aisle and Bird caught it. Bob Hulbert played first base and everything else inside the radius of his long arms and legs.

It has to be confessed that the red and white aggregation of the Tualco Chinooks showed the greater ability, but the "town boys" as the old settlers called the Snohomish contingent, were in good luck, and some of the players who, a week ago, could not have caught the measles, picked up long drives as though they had been strawberries. By the third inning the score stood 16 to 5 in favor of the "town boys."

At the end of the third inning *The Eye* man began to think of the ten mile ride behind him and before him. The perspiration evoked by the morning jaunt had struck in and the slightest movement had a painful penalty. Frank Evans had got there by a similar conveyance and was just as sore as the writer, so the two concluded to jump the game and hit the road.

The average reader in this western country has doubtless ridden horseback when he would have preferred to lie face downward over a sofa bed. Such a reader can imagine himself astride a hot and cruel saddle that felt as though it were stuffed with tacks, mounted on a horse with an upward and downward stroke resembling the excursions of a milk shaker. The agony lasted from half past three until six o'clock, when the reporter finally fell off the saddle in Elwell's stable.

The four-legged rascal cast a contemptous glare upon the writer

Snohomish vs. Everett

The First Game Ever Played by an Everett Base Ball Team

Six Innings Played Before the Everett Boys Got a Run

Score: Snohomish 39, Everett 5

Even with a crippled battery, a contemplative center field, and an unlucky third base, the Snohomish base ball players did up the Everett team yesterday and never soiled their new uniforms.

Snohomish went first to bat and knocked out two runs. In the next inning they scored 2, then 7, then 8, then a goose egg, then 4, and in the seventh inning every batter on the Snohomish team reached home plate, and Roll scored twice, making 10 in the inning. Oliver Thornton made the longest hit, and being anxious to make a home run, passed first base without touching it and was called out. Then Snohomish scored one in the eighth and 5 in the ninth for a total of 39.

Meanwhile, the Everett team came to bat seven times before they scored a run. At that point one of the Everett men aroused himself, sent a liner to left, and scored. Then every person in the crowd stood up and cheered and waved his hat. Even the Snohomish players swung their new caps in the air. In the eighth inning the Everetts scored twice, and twice again in the ninth. At present there is no ball ground in Everett, so the team has not been able to practice.

Some experts said it was not a good game, and that mistakes were too numerous. The worst error of the day, however, was committed by a dilatory or over-merciful providence which neglected to re-move from among the spectators two or three howlers who had lost control of their mouths and made 500 people weary with their bar-baric yawp. George Head took le-gal counsel to ascertain whether the instantaneous extinction of the youths would be regarded as justi-fiable homicide. He was instructed that it would not be homicide at all, but ordinary everyday retribu-tion. Appreciative remarks, well-timed applause and cheers at the right places, are always grateful to players; but perpetual hooting calls for something to drop on the of-fenders.

That Base Ball Game

Our Boys Beat the Sound's Crack Amateur Team

Snohomish people went to the ball game yesterday afternoon in a depressed state of mind, for they knew that Captain Roll, who plays second base, would not cavort about his accustomed place or steal any bases during the game. Mr. Roll was absent. So also was Campau who has done such val-iant work in left field. So the Snohomish people looked on gloomily when the home team went to bat and faced the fire throwers and accurate catchers of the Port Gamble aggregation.

Thrice did both sides come up before either made second base. Then McInnis of Port Gamble made a long streak and got to third. At this point the batsman swiped the ball with his wagon tongue and sent it off to the left of the base where McInnis stood. Gates, who was playing at that station for the Snohomish team, threw his mitten at the ball, while McInnis ran in. Everybody was surprised when Umpire Case called the ball a fair one and allowed the runner to score one for Port Gamble. There was protesting, of course, and Mr. Case was about to quit, when the Snohomish boys captured him and put him back again where he be-longed.

A man from Port Gamble swaggered through the crowd with a pocketful of money to bet on his team. He found no takers, though a short time afterwards Snohomish sports were looking for him with a microscope and discovered him not.

The game proceeded. (Seven-teen-year-old) Walter Thornton kept sailing the ball down the cen-ter aisle with a deceptive and elu-sive twist, before which the Port Gamblers went out in sad proces-sion.

The other club having set the example in the third inning, by scoring, Snohomish learned the route and Thomas got where he could read his title clear to a mark

Continued on next page

in Scorekeeper Fred Lysons' book. Yarnell followed suit and made two runs. Bob Hulbert likewise circumnavigated the field and had a run to his credit. This left the score: Port Gamble 1, Snohomish 4.

The visitors never got another run; in fact, the last three innings counted nothing for either side, and at an hour and forty-five minutes from the start the contest was finished.

Like other good games, this was nearly all played on the infield. Thornton and Morath did the work for the home team, and Lumsden and Clemens were almost as serviceable for the strangers. It will be observed that the catchers had but one passed ball each, while the pitchers are nearly tied on strikeouts. (Thornton 13, Lumsden 10) A big crowd was present, the day was hot and the game hotter. The Snohomish club promises to give another excursion to Port Gamble shortly. The visitors are the crack amateur team of the Sound, and this is said to be their first defeat.

There has ever existed a warm sociability between the Snohomish and Port Gamble teams, brought about through the many hotly contested games of early times.

Base Ball

Yesterday afternoon there was a scrub game at the Pastime Park grounds, a half dozen young men coming hither from Everett for practice. When Manager Bowen had divided the clubs and drawn on the spectators to fill out the sides, the diamond presented a very picturesque view. The players represented all stages of dress and undress and various conditions of uniform. They were equally varied as to size. Nate Raynor, who is six feet three or four in altitude, held down second base, while the Wohlgethan midget, with legs like a frog, supported him in right field. The weather was a trifle rheumatic, and spectators bunched themselves to keep warm, with the exception of the small boys, who found the top of the ten-foot fence the only place high and cold enough for them.

There were no surprising plays, but the work was rapid, the nine innings occupying about an hour. As closely as could be determined by guessing at half the score and multiplying the result by two, one side made seven runs and the other five. Bowen's decisions as umpire gave satisfaction to all concerned.

In another week the ground, which is at present somewhat tumular will be fenced and rolled into shape.

The Season Now Open

Everett Ball Players Take One from Snohomish

Champion Romancer Foss Beats All Previous Records of Eminent Liars

The base ball season opened yesterday when a nine came up from Everett and played the Snohomish boys. Our team was composed of a picked nine, some of whom were picked a little before they were ripe.

The spectators' interest was centered in the playing of Nate Raynor who plays first base for the Snohomish team. His reach is immense and his hands of such ample capacity that he has only to put them up in the form of a hopper and the ball disappears in their depths like a swallow diving into a chimney.

Owing to the condition of the grounds, which are soft and stony, there were few runs, the game closing with 5 to the credit of Everett, and 4 for Snohomish.

The audience got lots of fun out of the yarns volunteered by the professional liars in the crowd. Bill Foss, for instance, told how the game was played by the pioneers of Snohomish. The grounds then were near where Cedar Street is now. The left fielder, Foss said, took his position on School House Hill. The center fielder went out on Blackman's Lake in a canoe, while the right fielder covered the Machias Road on horseback. Games in those days usually lasted from 5 o'clock in the morning until 12 at night on account of the time wasted in hunting for balls that flew across the river on foul tips and landed on the bottom lands of South Snohomish. Foss averred that in one game he caught thirty-seven fly balls. When reminded by Lon Morgan that only twenty-seven flies caught could be necessary to win a game, Mr. Foss replied that his club always played nineteen innings.

The top of the fence was the only place high and cold enough

The center fielder went out on Blackman's Lake in a canoe

We Are the People!

Seatle Goes Down Before the Snohomish Nine

A Great Day for Walt Thornton

The story of yesterday's game should be told in howls, with the tooting of horns, the shouts of a multitude and the sound made by blowing across the mouth of a bottle. The Queen City of the Sound sent us her strong nine, who play under the name of the Teamsters, though it is said that a base ball team is the only team with which they have any intimate acquaintance. They had on crimson uniforms that looked as though they had been dyed in the blood of victims slain upon the field of battle. In their preliminary practice they batted the ball to the farthest field and the men stationed there caught it with unerring grip and flung it back to the home plate. The sphere flew from base to base and never touched the ground. The practice was away up and the Snohomish heart was away down. But the Snohomish Jays, in their sombre gray suits, showed up well in practice too, and went to the bat with the confidence of those who are unaccustomed to defeat.

The big audience held its breath while the Seattle pitcher sailed the ball down the center aisle. "Ball Four!" shouted the umpire, and there was tumult in the grand stand. It was Walter Thornton at the bat and he trotted to first base. Thornton stole second and ran to third when Roll followed with a single. Roberts hit a grounder to the pitcher and was thrown out at first. Roll misjudged the play, thinking Roberts had been caught out on a fly; he started back to first, saw the throw from the pitcher to the first baseman, called himself out and walked back to the player's bench. He was not touched by the ball and really isn't out yet. Raynor drove a long fly to the center fielder who muffed it, and when Thornton came home to score, the audience, in its joy tried to climb over itself, like bees swarming.

The visitors made a run and the acclamations were not so loud.

It was in the latter half of the second inning that the audience discovered that Walter Thornton was pitching great ball. The visitors could not touch him and he has the credit of winning the game. Ten men struck out, and only one base on balls, one wild pitch, and one man hit is an enviable record for a kid.

Clyde Scotney, the Snohomish mascot, arrayed in his miniature uniform, discharged faithfully the duties of his station.

The visitors brought along a shaggy little terrier which they expected would act as a hoodoo on their opponents, but the dog got rattled, misplaced his spell and went to sleep after the first inning.

The Teamsters played an even game and all the members were about equally responsible for the defeat of the team. They rallied strong in the ninth inning, and after a score had been made, they filled the bases with runners and only one man out. Then the man at bat popped a fly into Gates' hands. Gates jumped on third base with it, the runner couldn't get back and the struggle was ended, Snohomish winning 9 to 3.

The umpire, Amador Molino, was much admired, not only for his beauty, which is of the southern type, but also for the firmness with which he maintained his decisions, especially the erroneous ones.

The Teamster's shaggy dog got rattled and went to sleep

The Lord's Annointed

Children of Darkness Prevail Over Them

Seattle Meeteth a Sore Defeat

1. It came to pass in the days whereof we are bidden to write, that there existed in and about the Sound country many aggregations of athletic young men calling themselves ball teams.

2. Now among the cities of the Sound was a small town called Snohomish, and the same possessed a ball team whose members were the most skookum of all that country, and they know not what it was to be done up.

3. And they were goodly young men withal, saving in this, that they break the Sabbath with their ungodly game.

4. Now likewise, there was in the city of Seattle a club called the Athletics, which vaunted themselves that they could put up a better article of ball than the man who invented the game.

5. Hearing which, the skookum young men of Snohomish sent the Athletics word that they would give them a whirl, just for luck; and they sent a messenger to inquire what Sunday it would please the Seattle youths to joust with them.

6. But the Athletics said to the messenger, Go to; we are not heathen that we should play ball on Sunday; for they held that it was not lawful to indulge in sports on the Sabbath, lest the favor of the Almighty should be withheld.

7. So the young men of Snohomish took counsel among themselves and said, Verily, there are some which esteemeth one day above another, but unto us are they all alike for baseball purposes, and they swear by the horn spoon of Absalom, that they could wallop the Seattle aggregation any day of the week.

8. So they returned word that they would joust with the Queen City men on Saturday; and it was the eighth month and sixth and twentieth day; and the game was played.

9. Now there were in Snohomish many godly persons who had not attended any of the contests of the season because it was the Sabbath; but when they knew that there would be jousting on the seventh day (which is the Sabbath of nobody but the Lord thy God and a few sects without political influence), they said that they would attend. And the clergyman gathered from the contribution box a twobit piece which some careless worshiper had placed there, mistaking it for a button, and he went and sat in the high place which is called the grand stand, but the true name whereof is a lunatic asylum.

10. And when the young men from Seattle had broken bread, and drank wine, and crossed themselves, and offered up prayer, and spit on their hands, they girded up their loins and took the field.

11. And the Snohomish youths winked one to another, and exhorted each his neighbor to gin up.

12. The umpire said, Play ball, play ball; and the umpire said play ball.

13. So the pitcher cast the ball; and it came to pass that when the batsman, named Thornton, saw the ball approach, he smote it powerfully, so that it went to the shortstop, who found it too hot to hold, and Thornton got first base. Then followed Roll and Raynor, who hit the ball, albeit no score was made in that inning.

14. Then went Snohomish to the field and Seattle came to the bat, and the result thereof was a goose-egg.

15. But as the game waxed older, it began to appear that the Seattle boys were extraneous; yea, they were not in it, for the ungodly Snohomishers singed them hip and thigh, and they knew not where they were at.

16. And the strong arm of their pitcher was weakened, their batting order was broken up, their catcher got rattled and it seemed that the last one of them lost the number of his mess.

17. And the lunatics in the high place, called the grand stand, mocked them and counseled them each to return to his Sunday school class; the lunatics having no respect unto the conscientious scruples of the visitors.

18. So they were slaughtered and put to the rout, and were sore at heart and said that they would sell out damned cheap.

19. And among the lunatics in the high place was a young man, possessed of a devil and a tin horn, and he blew a devil of a blast upon the horn, and all went home. Whooplah!

Final score: Snohomish 14, Seattle Athletics 6.

The young men broke bread, drank wine, crossed themselves and offered up a prayer

That Sixth Inning

BY GEORGE MACDONALD

From first to last the lunatics
Displayed enthusiasm,
But there was joy when inning six
Convulsed them in a spasm;
For Gates hit way beyond third base,
And Anderson benignly
Smiled in the anxious pitcher's face
And lined one out so finely

That when Tom Bird came to the bat
The pitcher lost his cunning
And threw the ball so widely that
Tom got there without running.
Walt Thornton fired to center field
And crowded all the bases,
Next Roll came up and made an out
That left them in their places.
Then Raynor gave the sphere a crack
That counted as a double,
So all the boys to home got back
Without a bit of trouble.

And Morgan followed with a hit
That was a perfect drubber,
It sent the ball so far in space
That Raynor crossed the rubber.
'Twill long be known both far and wide
As that most famous inning
Which counted five for our team's side
And made us sure of winning.
When kids of each triumphant Jay
About his knees shall prattle,
He'll doubtless tell them of the way
Snohomish beat Seattle!

SNOHOMISH TRIBUNE • SNOHOMISH, WASHINGTON • SEPTEMBER 5, 1893

The Snohomish Invincibles Score Another Victory

Port Gamble Almost Shut Out

It Was the Best Game Yet Played On the Home Grounds

At twelve o'clock on Sunday the steamer *Henry Bailey*, having on board the Port Gamble ball club and about 50 excursionists, tied up to Fergusion's wharf at Snohomish. The attraction of the day was the ball game at Pastime Park, and when the game was called at 2:30, fully 600 people occupied seats in the grand stand and bleachers.

The Gamble boys had a professional battery with them and thought they had a walk-over—but they didn't. They wore pretty red suits and a confident air, and when they took the field for practice, they batted, caught long flies and picked up hot grounders like professionals. They played good ball, too, but their errors were costly ones, and Thornton kept the hits so well scattered that they only got one run in.

Horton pitched a strong game for Gamble, but Snohomish got nine safe hits and, with the help of some loose playing on the part of the visitors, managed to get eight runs in.

After the game the visiting ball tossers were escorted to the Poodle Dog Cafe where an elegant spread was awaiting them. The menu consisted of oyster soup, stuffed chicken, roast beef, roast mutton, boiled tongue, boiled ham, jelly and coconut cake; apple, custard and coconut pies; grapes, peaches, apples, pears and nuts; tea, coffee and milk.; string beans, tomatoes, green cucumbers and boiled potatoes; vanilla ice cream; and washed down with various kinds of mineral water and other bottled goods, to which everybody did ample justice.

The shrill whistle of the *Bailey* finally called the guests away, and with many a farewell cheer and cordial invitations to visit the mill town, the excursionists departed.

The visiting ball tossers were escorted to the Poodle Dog Cafe

The Championship Conceded

Oliver Thornton, secretary of the Snohomish base ball club, is in receipt of a communication from Secretary Ingersoll of the Seattle Athletic Association, stating that the Athletics will be unable to play our team at the Madison Street grounds next Monday.

Mr. Ingersoll says, in the first place, that it will be impossible for the Association to get up a team. They will not engage professionals, and their own club is disorganized. The catcher has business engagements, the pitcher's arm has given out entirely, the first baseman can't get off from work, the second baseman has gone to New York, and the others are all broke up.

In conclusion, Mr. Ingersoll says they will have to let the Championship rest with Snohomish until another season.

The Invincible Jays

At Last the Dream of Their Life is Realized

They Meet and Beat the Maroons

It Appears That There Is No Team In The State Able To Cope On Equal Terms With The Snohomish Nine—The Maroons Get Only Four Hits.

The people who attended the baseball game yesterday made a discovery, the which is, that the Snohomish club has been putting up the best ball played in the state. They have suspected all along that it was a pretty good article, and now they know it. Our club did up, by large majorities, the Ballards, the Company D team, the Teamsters and the Athletics, all of Seattle, besides scoring several minor victories, but all summer they have kept a bat in pickle for the Maroons, an aggregation of professional ball players who have cut out the work for all other clubs on the Sound. Yesterday the Jays took their wagon-tongue out of the brine and faced the stars. We are called upon once more to repeat that the result was as usual—Snohomish 10, Maroons 4.

The visitors were ball jugglers from away back. The catcher whom they brought with them is a crack player. To the scorer, he gave the name of Hines, but he is Wilson, who has been working this season in the California league. He is a big skookum man, with a professional air about him. He looked as if he might win the game alone, he was so expert; and when he tossed the ball in the air, caught it on the back of his hand and let it roll up his arm and down again, the sensation was something awful. He started in to superintend the ground by ordering Wally Anderson, who sat on the players' bench, to either keep still or get off the earth. Wally ran a nail through his foot at the Bakeman fire, and wears a big siwash sock in the place of a shoe, but he was not fazed. He told Wilson that he loved him, but had got to yip. He therefore yipped.

Zulu Bill Simmons, the Maroon pitcher, is a whizzer. His face is swarthy and calculated to inspire terror. If he were throwing the assagai of his native Zululand instead of a leather covered sphere, he couldn't do it any more wickedly than when he lets the ball go.

Then the visitors brought with them Mr. Pope, the all-round athlete, who is a champion at football and has a famous slide to first base. Also Babbitt, of Tacoma, the long distance batter; in fact, the northwest had been raked, as with a fine-tooth comb, to get together a combination that would give the Snohomish farmers what they need. This time, in announcing the game, the Seattle papers did not apologize or hedge. *The Post-Intelligencer* stated with directness that the Maroons were going to Snohomish to "cross bats" with the club at that place, and that a large delegation of their supporters and

Continued on next page

backers would accompany the club and cheer them on to victory.

The visitors were late and the game did not begin until 4 o'clock. The grand stand was crowded and a hundred people stood about the edge of the diamond. The game opened nervously, Snohomish going to bat and away from it without other result than the discovery that Zulu Bill was easy to hit. Then the Maroons came up and went back. They had also found out something, but it was not so satisfactory. They could hardly get a slice of the ball. Thornton pitched with speed and precision and with a most deceptive curve, while Bird did such good work behind the bat that he did not have an error or a passed ball.

The grand stand played without an error. When Thornton struck a man out the cranks jumped into the air and howled. When the Jays made three runs in the third inning, the lunatic asylum turned itself loose. Other runs by Snohomish in the fourth and fifth broke the backs of the Maroons, and they played the uphill game in a somewhat hopeless manner. It was almost dark when the ninth inning was reached. The spectators could not see the ball at all and the players saw it only when it went into the air. The darkness accounts for the three runs made by the visitors. The expiring effort of the Maroons was a pop fly. It settled in the hands of Gates and the game was over.

Some distinguishing features of the game were two three-base hits by Babbitt, a circus catch by Roberts, and Olie's luck in not having anything come his way.

Walter Thornton was struck behind the ear by a thrown ball at second base, and was stunned for a moment, but he recovered and pluckily pitched out the single inning which remained to be played.

The visitors were generous enough to admit that they had been beaten by the best club in the state.

Wilson, alias Hines, the catcher for the Maroons, was free to admit the cause for their defeat on Sunday. He said that when he stepped to the bat and Thornton pitched a ball at him he saw the object coming straight for his wagon-tongue and observed to himself, "This man is my meat and I will bat him beyond the city limits." Saying which he struck at the sphere, designing to hit it full in the face. "I think," added Mr. Wilson, "That I missed that ball by some fourteen inches."

Base Ball Melodrama

The sensational features so predominant in Sunday's base ball contest—i.e., the dramatical situations and climaxes—seemed so worthy a place on the stage, that were we capable we would undertake to dramatize just such a game. As we were perched on the bleachers, adding our individual screech to the general bedlam, at a most interesting period in the game (two men out, two on bases, and three balls, two strikes on the batter), a poetical "fan" near us remarked the beauty and expression of the scene presented on the diamond:

Walt Thornton standing like a Roman gladiator, proud in conscious strength; Morgan in a picturesque attitude only assumed by an alert ball-player; shapely Gates in a grandstand pose; Hennessey motionless as a marble form, and each and every man with his eye and mind upon one thing—the ball. At such a period, when not a murmur is heard in the grandstand and never a motion on the diamond save the nervous swaying of the batter's stick; and when Walt Thornton changes from a beautiful statue into a bewildering whirl of "south-paw" and a bullet-like delivery of the ball; when the batter braces himself for a supreme effort and makes one wild, vicious swipe at the flying sphere, only to hear it "BIFF" in Tommy Bird's big mitt—what a pregnant silence follows — a silence so deep that the busted "rooters" on a neighboring roof could distinctly hear the umpire's "Batter Out!" — then how suddenly the scene changes— what an easing up of nerve-tension and opening out of lungs in one wild tumultuous yell of delight.

Could such a scene be truthfully portrayed on the stage the actors certainly would never have cause to complain of lack of enthusiasm in the audience!

(Snohomish 10, Seattle Maroons 4; Thornton struck out 12.)

Seattle is Victorious

But Port Gamble and the Umpire Won the Game

The Curtain Rose Upon a Fight

A Seattle Delegation Got Into Trouble With Ticket-Taker Booth, Who Was Proceeding to Thrash the Same When Interrupted by Center Fielder Rogers.

They scratched and hit
And gouged and bit
   And tumbled in the mud.
Till all the ground
For yards around
   Was covered with their blood;
And piles of noses, ears and eyes
Arose like pyramids to the skies.

Sunday's ball game had a prologue which made it one of the most interesting events of the season. The new feature was a free and easy fight, started by two drunken young men from Seattle. The visiting team got here quite early in the day, so that their sympathizers and supporters who came along with them had time to see the town and brace up for the afternoon's amusement. The two drunken young men from Seattle, and an older man who encouraged them in all sorts of deviltry, beat their way to seats in the grand stand, and procuring a bottle with the bottom knocked out, started in to make things hideous with hootings, tootings and indecent language. Billy Booth, who was ticket taker for the day, asked them to desist, reminding them that they had not paid for the privilege of sitting in the grand stand; that there were ladies present, and that disorderly conduct could not be tolerated. He followed up his remarks by touching one of the hobos on the shoulder and ordering him off the benches. The man replied by attempting to strike Booth in the face. As is well known, Mr. Booth's blood has been warmed by a tropical climate and he is not a safe man to hit in an offhand, miscellaneous manner. The result which followed was what the bystanders expected, and in less time than is required to relate the circumstances of the transaction, the atmosphere was full of legs and arms attached to the persons of the young men. The fight would have been a very brief incident if Teamster Rogers, who came to play center field, had not conceived the idea that he was born to illustrate the beatitude which pronounces a benediction on peace-makers, his system of restoring order being to thrash the first man conveniently at hand.

It was a glorious shindy which ensued. In pursuance of his peaceful policy, Mr. Rogers assailed Booth, with evident intent to do him bodily harm. As Booth was already beset by two persons, this looked eminently unfair to Stenographer Ferguson, who took sides with Booth and got hit by Rogers. The writer of shorthand gave Rogers the best he had in the shop and shattered a large and valuable cane over the ball player's skull. A moment later Rogers had Ferguson's head in chancery and struck him twice in the face. Subsequent proceedings interested Ferguson no more. On or near this date Hank Kennedy got tangled up in the fracas. He had a shillala, and was in his glory. Pretty soon the friends of Rogers took the eminent center fielder out of harm's way. His Maroon shirt had lost a sleeve, and he had injuries about the head which evidently affected his brain, for it took four or five substantial persons to hold him and they were not very successful in performing that duty.

A photograph of the scene taken at this point would have shown probably a score of excited individuals paired off or bunched in groups of four or five, gesticulating wildly, occasionally striking a blow or attempting to end the trouble by making it worse. Such a view would also have discovered Mr. William Booth wearing a smile like a harvest moon or like a slice of melon or like almost anything else large enough and curved enough to represent the grin of a man who has come out of a fight unhurt and can calmly watch his opponents fighting one another.

None of the ball players except Rogers took any part in the trouble, and his getting mixed up in it was, as before stated, due to his desire for peace. The rest went out in the diamond and practiced. The scrimmage, which was over in ten minutes, could not have been at all funny to those who got hurt, but to the recorder of events who sat on the top shelf of the grand stand and watched developments, it was

Continued on page 43

Before the game there was a free and easy fight

worth several weeks of peaceful life. All who looked on express deep regret that Booth was not let alone when the two blackguards attacked him.

After these preliminaries, play was called, Zulu Bill Simmons filling out the Seattle team which had been rendered shorthanded by the foregoing occurences. Rogers went and sat in the grand stand, refusing to participate further in the day's proceedings.

Snohomish went first to bat and Roll scored a run. Then they shut out the visitors for five innings and were four times shut out themselves. In the sixth Morgan got around and the score stood 2 to 0 in favor of the home team. Once the Teamsters had two men on bases and again had the bases full, but Thornton's curves deceived the batsmen who followed and the five men got no further. Before the sixth was over Harris, the big left fielder, broke the ice and came home. Afterwards our amateurs could do nothing against the precise play of the professionals, who made one run in the seventh and two in the ninth. The hot pace was too much for the kid battery. Bird lost his luck, and Thornton's arm got weary, and so the Snohomish Jays were defeated, 4 to 2.

From the list of players it will be seen that the Teamsters had Port Gamble's battery, Horton and Blanford, and that the other players were picked out of the principal clubs of the state. The umpire probably tried to be fair, but he gave Snohomish the worst of it on decisions, which may have discouraged the boys.

Amateur Base Ball

The end of the baseball season emphasises the fact that amateur baseball is a thing of the past. Scarcely a club in the Northwest has been entirely free from professionalism. There are two causes for this inability to keep the sport on an amateur basis.

The first of these is the importance of one man out of the nine. Given an extra good pitcher, one club will win whether the rest of the team is up to the standard or not. The result is a strong temptation for the club which has no good twirler to import one.

The other cause is this: It is so hard to develop a first class player from raw material that the clubs are tempted to go out to the surrounding country and pick up developed players, thus defeating the prime object of the amateur athletic clubs, viz: the development and enjoyment of athletic sport among their members.

The only way to overcome this is by constantly introducing new games. La Crosse, Bowling and Golfing are not open to these objections. For several seasons at least they would be good live amateur sports, no one knowing who would have the best team until the games were played. La Crosse is said to be a great game. It ought to be introduced.

The Multnomah Club vanquished its bitter rival, the Portland Amateur Athletic Club (doubtfully amateur) in the game of baseball last Saturday, and is entitled to the championship of the Northwest.

Chapter Two: Baseball Games, 1900-1905

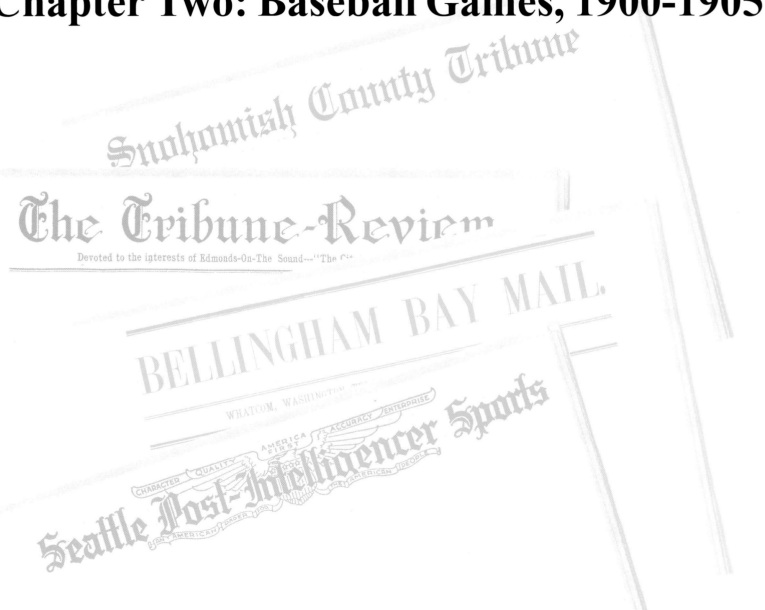

Beaten by Bloomers

Our Local Giants Defeated by the Boston Maids

Saturday, June 30th, one of the greatest ball games Snohomish people ever witnessed was played at Baseball Park. Local lights were first on the ground for practice, which made a decisive change in the betting in favor of the home team. The Bloomers came next with five minutes of practice, evidently for the purpose of locating the low places in the field. The game was called at 3:15 sharp with the Bloomers at the bat. Pitcher Moran raised the once white sphere and like a skyrocket it bounded toward the frail maiden with the bat. She immediately fanned the air. Strike one! said Umpire Betzig, and the chances looked blue for the Boston Bloomers. Once more Moran, the terrible, landed another over the plate and strike two was called. The excitement at this point was intense. Catcher Ebert silently donned the muzzle and stealthily crept to within three feet of the unsuspecting maiden with the bat. A high ball was ordered. The bat-

ter made a terrific smash and connected. She fairly flew to first which was presided over by "Long Billy" Smith, who in getting out of the way ran against the fence. On, on, the maiden sped, until she arrived at second panting and out of breath, where Umpire Betzig, as gently as possible, informed her she had connected with Catcher Evert's head instead of the ball. By request of Moran she was called out.

Boston Bloomer No. 2, a tall blond girl with blood in her eye, walked complacently to the bat. Moran with a ghost-like grin let go his awful right arm. The ball, like lightning, came twirling toward the plate when biff came the tall girl's bat and landed the ball over the fence. She made a home run and a recess was declared for 15 minutes while the fielders looked for the ball. They reported the ball lost and the Bloomers were given three runs for the hit they had made.

Two more runs were piled up for the Bloomers and the bases were all full when Sarah Bernhardt

came to bat, fanned the ball twice and knocked a fly to left fielder Ferguson, who caught it and with a straight liner to home put out the runner from 3rd, thus making the first double play in five long and weary years.

Home boys came to the bat while the maids tripped gaily to the field through the dog fennel. Moran was up to the bat with his left eye on Lilly Langtry, the South Paw pitcher. She landed three balls over the plate and the umpire promptly called three strikes and Pitcher Moran was out. He objected, saying he was not looking for the ball so soon, but the umpire's decision was sustained. Sammy Knapp was the next victim who threw his bat at the ball and was ruled out for his viciousness. Next came Catcher Ebert with a bandage over his right eye, who reached first base on balls. Smith was the next to face the South Paw wonder. The ball was poised for an instant before delivery when Coacher Moran ordered his man to make a fierce run for second. Instead of the ball going over the plate as always before, with the swiftness of a streak of chain lightning it went to first and out went poor Ebert. Score, Bos-

ton Bloomers 5; Giants 0.

This was a fair sample of the playing throughout the game, but space forbids us giving the fight by rounds, so we skip those intervening and take up the last. In this Sarah Bernhardt was first to the bat. She hit it hard, knocking Sherman Moody off the roof of a nearby house, fracturing his arm in 13 places. It was called a foul and she went out. Omene and Maxine Eliott made two more runs and Brigham Young Roberts, the Mormon catcher, made three more, making 14 runs before the side was retired to give the Giants a show.

Joe Altman came to bat, knocked a liner and made first base. Ebert next limped to the bat, fanned the air and was called out amid loud applause from the gallery. Sammy Knapp reached first on an error by a spectator, who was promptly arrested for so doing. "Long Billy" Smith made up his mind to hit the ball, but did not see the hole in his bat. Moran came next, made a foul and the ball was lost and the game called off.

Final score, about 15 or 20, to 2 or 3 in favor of the Bean Eaters.

Burlesque Baseball

Boston Bloomers Have But Three Ball Players With Them

Rest of the Team Give Very Poor Exhibition—Badly Beaten

"You can't tell me, young man," said a middle-aged gentleman on an Oak Bay (British Columbia) bound car yesterday afternoon, "that a girl can bat and throw a ball just like a man."

"Well, they can," replied the young man, "else how could the Bloomers get away with Seattle and Winnipeg, and come near beating Vancouver, too?"

"Oh! I can quite understand the Bloomers nearly winning from Vancouver, but, seriously! young man, would you stand behind your wife and let her take a shot with a boot-jack at two feline disturbers of the peace on the back alley fence?"

The young man blushingly stammered that he hadn't a wife, but he had heard that a stone thrown by a girl always went in the opposite direction to that aimed at.

The above is a sample of the numerous discussions that took place in Victoria on the mooted point whether girls could play baseball like men, and it was to set all doubts at rest that hundreds of men dropped business worries yesterday afternoon and went out to the Oak Bay grounds to see the Boston Bloomers play with the Victoria team.

The grand stand was also crowded with the fair sex, and, with pardonable pride, they were looking forward to demonstrate to the men folk that they weren't the only pebbles on the beach.

Psychologically then, the men were sceptical, the ladies were hopeful. The question was one of absorbing scientific interest, for, if the Bloomers approximated all the flattering advance notices, then champions of the equality of the sexes would have a brand new argument, and women would soon be vying with men in the athletic arena. Everyone went out to the grounds.expecting to finally dispose of the question whether women could adapt themselves to the popular pastime of baseball, and everyone came away feeling disappointed, for the problem still hovers in the realm of uncertainty, and the student of feminine potentialities can only conjecture. If Maud and Lucy, who alternated in the positions of pitcher and short-stop are really girls, then everyone is prepared to concede that girls with practice could throw and bat like boys. Despite their girlish locks and falsetto voices, they looked, ran and acted like men, and most of the audience were disposed to catalogue them as good female impersonators. Maud and Lucy, whether men or women, are great ball players; in fact, they and Sheppard, the undisguised male catcher, were the whole team, for the rest of the players, who were unmistakably girls, could not catch, throw or bat, and would be a mark for any team of twelve year old youngsters.

The regular first basewoman or baseman was on the sick list, and the accommodating "Pat" Deasy was selected to fill the position. A glance at the error column will show that "Pat" should travel as a Bloomer girl. If "Pat" were to don bloomers, shave his upper lip, and deck his top piece with flowing blond curls, no one would dream of putting him down for a man, for he can make as many errors as the poorest of the Bloomers.

Holness, the Victoria pitcher, passed through the trying ordeal of being tempted by the most bewitching smiles. The Bloomers favored him with their sweetest glances, but he was proof against all feminine wiles, and instead of lobbing the ball over the plate, he made it fairly whistle as it shot past the poor Bloomers. As to the game itself, it was a wretched burlesque, although the work of Maud and Lucy was of the pyrotechnic order, the fielding of Maud in the first four innings evoking rounds of applause. Both Maud, the southpaw twirler, and Lucy had great speed, and quick shoots, but the Victorias had little difficulty in solving their delivery. The home club could have made the score 30 to 1 if they had desired, for in the last few innings they went out on purpose, else they might be batting yet. Gypsy's catch in center field must not be forgotten. There is no question about Gypsy being a woman, and it was a creditable feat, but hardly worth 85 cents (10 cents car fare, 50 cents admission, and 25 cents grand stand) to see.

In the oft repeated words of Barnum, the people love to be humbugged, but for unadulterated imposition the so-called Bloomer girls take the bun.

Final score: Victoria 22, Boston Bloomers 1.

1901 Everett Baseball Team

The 1901 team was arguably the best baseball team the city of Everett has ever had. They won their first 27 games in a row. There were three professional teams in Washington—Seattle, Tacoma and Spokane—and Everett beat them all by shutouts. Vancouver, B.C. finally broke Everett's win streak.

At that time Everett was classified as an amateur team, although we would have called them "semi-pros." Tickets were sold for the games and the gate receipts were split between the two teams, usually 50-50. After taking out expenses, each team would distribute its share to their players based on an agreed percentage, i.e., the star pitcher would get more than the reserve catcher.

Everett did not play in a league in 1901, but they had no trouble scheduling opponents. Because of their success on the field they attracted large crowds, so their opponents could count on a big payday. For the professional league teams, playing Everett made an extra payday in addition to their regular league salaries.

The Everett team was led by former Major Leaguer Walter Thornton (see player bio) who acted as Captain and Manager. He played first base and batted over .500 for the season. (The entire team, including pitchers, batted over .300) Thornton was so popular in Everett that in November a front page headline in the *Everett Daily Herald* proposed "Thornton For Mayor." The next day he declined on the grounds that the nomination should go to an older, more experienced citizen. Walter Thornton was 26 years old.

The star pitcher was Fred Schoch (see player bio). Originally from Iowa, he was signed by Everett out of the University of Washington. Schoch pitched the shutouts against the three professional teams. He took over as Manager of the Everett team after Walter Thornton resigned in September.

After the season the team was feted at a splendid banquet complete with speeches, toasts, and responses from Schoch and Thornton. The players were presented with gold rings appropriately engraved to commemorate their great season.

Back Row, *far left: Fred Schoch.* **Man in bowler,** *William Haferkorn, team president.* **Front Row**, *second from left: Walter Thornton*

Woodmen's Team

Was Hypnotized at Snohomish by the Collection of Feminine Sweetness Collected in the Grandstand

"We were badly done up over there, but it was not the Snohomish club that really beat us, although they play good ball. But the grandstand was simply packed with the sweetest aggregation of girls that ever got together, and under the circumstances the boys could scarcely be blamed for not playing ball. It must have been a putup job. We were hypnotized, razzle-dazzled, put clear out of business by the flower garden behind the screen. Every member of the team swears that he will come back to Snohomish to live as soon as our trip is ended. In fact, I had to drag them out of town by brute strength, and I fear a wholesale desertion before I can get the lovesick sphere chasers back on their native bunchgrass."

(Interview with the manager of the Spokane Woodmen baseball team after they lost to Snohomish, 16 to 6.)

Win Kind Words

Everett's Baseball Experts Pleased the Victoria People Though They Beat Them 10 to 5.

Of Tuesday's game at Victoria the *Victoria Daily Times* has the following to say of the Everett team:

"As was expected the crack Everett team played tag with the local nine. The Victorians apparently suffered from a very severe case of stage fright during the opening innings of the game, the easiest fly balls being dropped by the fielders, and all hands seemed anxious to outdo one another in a general muffing contest. The visitors, on the other hand, played star ball. The great Schoch held the locals down in fine style, except in the sixth and seventh innings, when the home team scored all of their runs.

"The largest crowd that assembled to witness a baseball game in Victoria in years attended the match, and judging by the amount of applause and cheering in the stands they were thoroughly pleased with the afternoon's sport. No doubt many present expected the Victoria boys to win, but when one stops to consider that the home boys are merely amateurs and the visitors have on their team several celebrated ex-professionals, the final outcome of the game was no more than could be expected.

"The feature of the game was the pitching of the visitor's big twirler Schoch, who certainly is all that he is claimed to be, his speed at times being simply terrific, and his control perfect, while his slow low ball is one of the most deceptive imaginable. Pringle caught a fair game, but seems to have some trouble in holding Schoch's hard straight ball. Thornton played first base about as well as has been seen here in a long while, and the balance of the visitors' team all put up a good hard game.

"At the bat the Everett boys were 'crack-a-jacks.' They started at Holness in the first inning as though they intended knocking him out of the box. Singles and doubles followed in rapid succession, and when the side was retired a big three showed on the score board. Law led the batting on his side with three singles, Thornton with a single and a double coming next.

"The game was a good one from a spectator's standpoint, being full of hitting and sharp fielding. The Everett team is a most gentlemanly one, and put up good clean ball; rowdy work and squabbling with the umpire being not in their line."

To Play Three Games Tomorrow

Game Will Be Played At Stanwood In Morning
Stanwood and Anacortes Teams To Be Here In Afternoon

First on the program tomorrow is a game between the Everett and Stanwood teams at Stanwood. The Everett team leaves here at 9:30 for a game at Stanwood at 11:30, after which it will bring the Stanwood team together with some 200 excursionists down here, arriving at 3:20. The first game here will be called at 3:30 and the game with Anacortes will be called immediately after the first is finished.

The Anacortes team will come down on the steamer *Swinomish* with an excursion of 250 to 300 rooters, and expects to arrive here between noon and 2p.m. Dean and Brown in the Anacortes lineup are the old Bellingham battery, seen here a number of times this year. It will also be remembered that Dean pitched a game for Everett against Sedro-Woolley.

The games here will be contested at the fair grounds, and one admission of 25 cents will be charged to both games.

These two excursions will bring some 350 to 400 people to town, and Everett hotels and restaurants will have a chance to tax their capacity and quick service.

The Everett bunch is out to win all three games, and if the Everett fans will do their share of the rooting, Everett will certainly win out.

Held Up In Everett

A bold midday robbery occured in Everett last Sunday afternoon, just a few hours after the arrival of the steamer *Swinomish* from Anacortes with the baseball excursion. Shortly after the noon luncheon the Anacortes delegation repaired to the baseball grounds where they expected to meet a friendly delegation of Everett gentlemen to welcome them as visitors to the city and to show them a good time. Instead they were met by nine river-front thugs who held them up and robbed them of a ball game. If Anacortes owed the Devil 75 thoroughbred stinkers and his satanic majesty took that Everett umpire as full payment for the debt, Satan would lose his money.

The game was a good one and by rights should have been five to one in favor of Anacortes, but the Everett thugs and their umpire tool deliberately stole the game, disgusting even their own citizens who watched the bold holdup and pronounced it a downright robbery on the part of the home team. When protests were made to the umpire by the Anacortes team, the Everett thugs from the waterfront would get in the fight and when the umpire would not willingly decide in their favor, they would make him do so. Had Anacortes made a dozen home runs they would have been counted out. No visitors, not even the Siwash teams from the reservation were ever given such a rotten deal as were the Anacortes boys at Everett last Sunday. Nine tenths of the crowd present declared the game won by the Anacortes boys and lost only through highway robbery committed by an imbecilic umpire and nine waterfront hold-ups.

UpAgainst the Real Thing

Everett Wins Ball Game in a Walk—
Many Broken Sports Now in the City

Anacortes went up against the real thing when they tackled Everett in a baseball game at Athletic Park Monday afternoon. Our boys can play some ball, but they are not exactly in the same class with Everett, and on Monday the fool and his money soon parted.

Everett did not send over her Bowery toughs this time or the nine reformed greatly, for surely they were a fine, gentlemanly lot of boys, and the way they could play ball was a caution to cats. The Anacortes boys won from Mt. Vernon, Seattle, Bellingham, Fort Casey, La Conner and other teams, and had become some pumpkins at baseball, so much so that many citizens were eager to back the home team against Everett and did so, but today they are only broken sports, for Everett slathered the home team in a horrid fashion and won about $400. They didn't hold the boys up this time, just played a legitimate game and walked off with the swag, and now the man with the sore spot stands on the street corner and tells how the play came up. Many think the thing was a put up job, and we guess it was on the part of Everett and a right clever job at that, for certainly their team work was lightning and they showed that while Anacortes could play good ball, they were simply playing out of their class. Our boys, however, have put up the finest game and played the best ball all through the season of any team the city has ever had.

Final score: Everett 9, Anacortes 3

Baseball Mutiny

September 6: **Baseball Players in Rank Mutiny**

Go to Anacortes Without Manager's Knowledge

There was no baseball game yesterday for the Labor Day celebration at Electric Park because the Everett team mutinied and went to Anacortes instead. The Bothell team arrived on time, but the Everett players were miles away.

Manager Dresen knew nothing of the intended action of his wards until about noon yesterday when he went to the grounds at Electric Park. Then he found his team had vanished with all the necessary paraphernalia for playing ball.

The "vanishing" was the result of a plot which the players kept carefully to themselves. They made arrangements for the game, hired a launch and went to Anacortes, leaving yesterday morning at 5 o'clock.

They had planned the trip for several days. Not one of them intimated to the manager that the trip was going to be made, so the Bothell men could not be stopped.

The latter were wroth when they found out the state of affairs. The Bothell players were not even paid their expenses.

September 7: **Baseball Team Now in Trouble**

Catcher Waters Under Arrest On Charge of Embezzlement of Paraphernalia

Everett's baseball team is in trouble. Emil Waters is under arrest, charged with embezzlement of ten baseball suits, a catcher's chest protector, mask and mitt, the whole being of a value more than enough to constitute the crime of embezzlement.

The whole trouble arose over the disappearance of the team when it was scheduled to play at Electric Park on Labor Day, and a deep laid plot to accomplish the overthrow of the former manager of the team, John Dresen.

According to the story told by the new manager of the team, B. Cecil Jack, there was good and ample reason for members of the team being "sore." He claims that the boys had not been treated right at any time; that Manager Dresen had not lived up to his contract with them, and had refused to pay them the salary promised.

Continued on page 55

Catcher Waters under arrest for embezzlement of paraphernalia

When members of the team failed to show up on Labor Day, Manager Dresen was puzzled. He could not understand their absence, nor could he ascertain where they had gone until last evening when it was reported that they had gone to Anacortes to play there on Labor Day, the launch *Marguerite* having been chartered for the purpose.

That was puzzle number two, for how members of the team could secure the vessel without paying cash was a puzzle to everybody at all familiar with baseball players generally, for they are here today and gone tomorrow. But the unexpected happened, and there are people in town who are still puzzled as to who put up the money to hire that boat.

This morning Manager Dresen met Emil Waters, who is said to have charge of the property of the team during the absence of Manager Dresen, and demanded of him the catcher's outfit, consisting of a chest protector, mask and catcher's mitt. He was informed by Waters that he did not know where the outfit was.

That settled all peaceable efforts on the part of Manager Dresen. He at once decided to take steps to recover his property, and as Waters had been left in charge

of it he at once went to Prosecuting Attorney Cooley and stated his case. It required but a short time to draw up a complaint which was presented to Justice McLaren, and a warrant was issued.

When the necessary legal document had been prepared for the arrest of Waters it was turned over to Deputy Sheriff Beard who sallied forth in quest of his prey. Waters was located on Hewitt Avenue and placed under arrest.

After the arrest of Waters Manager Dresen let drop the remark that "this is but the beginning," and that other developments will follow.

That had the effect of a Japanese bomb falling into Russian ranks, for mentally, at least, the "bunch" was put to rout. They did not know exactly how far they were liable, but feared possible consequences.

And that is where the baseball team of Everett is today. They have a new manager, but whether or not he is in position to issue checks for their salary when called upon to do so is another question.

It is also entirely another question as to whether or not the public will be disposed to lend its support to a team which has deliberately planned to throw everybody

down when every man knew that a game was scheduled for Electric Park on Labor Day.

September 8: **Baseball Team is Turned Down**

One of the prominent business men in speaking of the action of the team in throwing down the people of Everett said: "That was one of the dirtiest tricks I ever saw played. I do not care anything about Manager Dresen personally, but he has worked hard to keep a baseball team going in this town and has succeeded when teams in all surrounding cities have quit early in the season. I do not think that he is the greatest baseball manager that ever happened, but he stands head and shoulders above the whole bunch of players now calling themselves the Everett baseball team. And they have no more right to call themselves 'Everett' when they play away, or even here, than they have to call themselves Tacoma or 'Frisco. They are nothing but a disgruntled and discredited bunch of baseball players who do not appear to want to do the square thing.

"Citizens should drive them out of town. We do not wish such people here unless they go to work

like others and make an honest living for themselves. In the meantime they should be enjoined in the courts from appearing anywhere as the Everett baseball team."

September 9: **Waters Case Now On Before the Court**

Attorney Robert Hulburt
Defends Ball Player

This morning in justice court the case of the State against Emil Waters, on the charge of embezzlement, was before the bench.

When time arrived for hearing the case the whole baseball bunch was in the court room and sneers and jeers flew thick and fast when Manager Dresen entered the room. That seemed to spur Prosecuting Attorney Cooley to greater efforts to establish his case against Waters.

The whole of the forenoon was taken up on an examination of Manager Dresen, the evident object of the examination by Attorney Hulbert being to establish ownership of the suits, and in an effort to convey the inference that they had been purchased with proceeds of baseball games played since the team was organized.

Notwithstanding repeated efforts on the part of Attorney

Continued on next page

Hulburt, Manager Dresen maintained that he, and he alone, was responsible for the team; that he hired, paid and fired the players at will, and that none of them had at any time claimed the suits in question, even when discharged from the team or when other players were secured temporarily in their places. He also produced bills and checks to show that he had personally paid for the material used for the suits as well as the caps and stockings.

A sharp colloquy occured between Messrs. Cooley and Hulburt during the hearing, the latter insisting upon direct answers to questions which the witness maintained could not be answered without qualification and which he insisted on explaining. Mr. Hulburt absolutely insisted upon questions being so answered while Prosecuting Attorney Cooley informed the witness that he might answer questions to suit himself, regardless of what Attorney Hulburt might say; Manager Dresen continued to qualify his answers.

Emil Waters was the next witness placed on the stand and he testified as to his understanding of the ownership of the suits. He said that he believed that the "club" owned the suits and that they had a right to take them to Anacortes or any other place.

Questioned regarding B. Cecil Jack being manager, he said that a meeting of the "club" had been held and a new manager elected. Asked regarding the amount they were to be paid he said they were to play on a percentage basis under the management of B. Cecil Jack.

Regarding the trip to Anacortes, Waters said he did not know until early the morning they left that a trip was to be made to Anacortes and then someone came to his door and awoke him, saying that the team was to go to Anacortes right away. That was the first he knew of any such plan.

Asked as to where the suits in question are, Waters said that he had no knowledge where any of them are except the one which he wore, and that is at present in his room.

September 10: **Catcher Waters Is Bound Over**

Bonds Are Furnished
by William Haferkorn.
Everett's Catcher is at Liberty.

Emil Waters was bound over to Superior Court by Justice McLaren this morning in the sum of $200 on the charge of embezzlement of the base ball suits worn by players who have constituted the Everett team during the present season.

September 9, 1904

Peace Warrants Issued for Two

Threaten a Reporter of the Everett Herald
One is Now Under Arrest
Object to Article Published in the Herald and Threaten to Retaliate.

This forenoon one of the reporters of the *Herald* went to the cigar store of William Haferkorn with a view of securing the names of those baseball men who left the people of Everett in the lurch and went to Anacortes. There he encountered B. Cecil Jack, the new manager of the team, and Charles Gabey, both of whom took strenuous exception to the story published in the *Herald* last evening. In connection therewith they made dire threats against the reporter, saying that they would "knock his block off" and other things which are generally accepted to mean trouble for the person against whom they are directed. "I fixed one reporter so that he never mentioned my name again," Gabey said, "and the next time I go at one of the cheap skates I will make him a fit subject for the undertaker."

Mr. Gabey was informed that his name was not sacred to the newspaper fraternity when it came up in a public way. Then Gabey turned and said, "I am giving you warning now that unless I am let strictly alone by you cheap guys that some of you will be in the hands of the undertaker, and as you admit that you wrote the article last night, that applies to you!"

"You have made a public threat against my life, and I shall take steps to protect myself, even securing a permit from the chief of police to carry a gun," said the reporter, whereupon the controversy ended.

Not wishing trouble of any kind, the *Herald* reporter went to the Prosecuting Attorney and secured a warrant for the arrest of both Gabey and Jack. At the time of going to press only Mr. Gabey had been apprehended.

We Told You So

Stanwood Defeated the Rainiers of Seattle, 7 to 1

Stanwood Now Claims the Amateur Championship of Puget Sound.

"The ball game played last Sunday between Billy Belond's nine of Seattle and the Stanwood team was a complete victory for Stanwood. Those who came to witness the game will remember for a long time the drubbing that the Rainiers received at the hands of our boys.

"Our boys played fast ball and Billy's team was up against the real thing from the beginning to the end. In fact, the Rainiers were so far outclassed that Stanwood made monkeys of them all the way.

"Sunday morning the Rainiers came into town with their manager, Billy Belond, who, like one of ancient Rome's gladiators drove to the ball park there to be vanquished from the arena with his ill fated matchless ball team. Billy and his man Friday who kept the official score showed that they were not sports at all. For leaving the ball grounds beaten, disappointed and crestfallen, they went their way to Seattle and deliberately misrepresented the game and result of the playing in the sporting page of *The Seattle Times:* 'Billy Belond, affectionately known as Billy the Mug, took his scrappy little Rainier team to Stanwood yesterday and trimmed the hard hitters of that burg to the tune of 7 to 1...'

"The above bit of rot shows how keenly Billy took his defeat here Sunday, and unlike a genuine sport, bolstered up his crushing defeat by deliberately falsifying the result of the game...

"The game was fast from the beginning and the best that was ever played in this section of the country and would be considered as good a game as any played by the league teams. The boys were all in trim, up on their metal (sic), and played ball that made Billy the Mug turn green with envy.

"Dode Brinker pitched a fine game of ball and the Seattle lineup got only five safe hits off him during the game."

That little burg Stanwood got no respect from the big city-slickers in Seattle. The *Seattle Post-Intelligencer* also got the game result reversed. *The Seattle Star* got the winner right but misspelled the town name as "Stanhope."

Opening Day • May 11, 1905

Caption under front page newspaper photo*: This picture gives a fair idea of the crowd of baseball enthusiasts that attended the opening game of the season on the Everett home grounds. It was the greatest crowd ever assembled at a ball game in Everett. Every business of importance in the city closed early and the few that kept open might as well have shut up shop for all the business they did . A number of sawmills shut down at noon and gave their employees a half day holiday for this occasion. Practically one forth of the population of the entire city witnessed the game.* The Everett Smokestackers lost the game 9 to 3, but rebounded to capture the 1905 Northwest League championship in a 97 game season. 1905 was the first and only season Everett had a professional baseball team until 1984 when the Bavasis brought the rookie league Giants to town.

Hidden Ball Trick

Yesterday in Everett, Bellingham edged out the home team in a hard fought league game, 1 to 0. The only score was made in the second inning on an error by the Everett third baseman.

In the seventh, Kelsey, the Bellingham left fielder made a sensational running catch of Altman's long drive which appeared to be headed out of the ball grounds.

From the grandstand the catch appeared to be a phenomenal one. No one believed Kelsey had caught the ball until he turned around and without stopping threw it in to the infield.

Toward the end of the game the clouds had lowered so thickly that a lantern was necessary to see the ball, and from the grandstand things had begun to assume a blurred look.

However, H. Mulholland and a number of other Snohomish fans were out near left field and they say that Kelsey did not catch the ball at all. One of them said this morning: "We saw the left fielder deliberately take a ball from his shirt and throw it in after Altman's fly had passed over him by at least twelve inches. It was a trick worth seeing. Darkness and 'gall' permitted and prompted the play, and it probably cost Everett the game. The dumbfounded trio, Manager Hulen, Heitmuller, and Altman held a consultation near first base immediately after the catastrophe and couldn't figure out what hit them."

Snohomish fans don't particularly love Everett, but they hated to see Altman, a Snohomish native, robbed of a hit that in all probability would have changed the fortune of the game.

Hidden ball trick

McCloskey Will Protest and Claim the Pennant

Vancouver Manager McCloskey's vocal organs have resumed their functions after a three days' rest.

His anger at President Haferkorn and Manager Hulen of Everett continues unabated, however.

McCloskey relieved his mind in an interview at Vancouver yesterday. He is going to claim the pennant for the first series for his team, he says. He claims to have proof that Hulen was in cahoots with Manager Drennan of Bellingham and that the latter threw the Sunday morning game to Everett.

McCloskey will enter a protest against the match at a meeting of the league to be called by Vancouver for this purpose. "Honest" John also claims that he had an agreement with Hulen that the season should end with the Sunday session and that this agreement was binding under the constitution of the league. A further claim is made that Haferkorn deceived League President Lucas by misinforming the latter.

McCloskey apparently is not going to take his medicine gracefully. He is writing pieces for the papers and in an epistle to the *Seattle Times* he says:

"Think of a special train in a bush league! Had I turned a trick like that they would have bellowed about McCloskey, the spendthrift, who will stand at no expense to win a pennant. Bush leaguers riding on a special train!

"Vancouver won that first half fair and square, and yet we are put out of it by a special train in a bush league when we need every dollar to make ends meet and finish the season. I was forced to weaken my team on account of all the talk about exceeding the salary limit or the race would not have been close, and after all that for the good of the league I am robbed of the pennant by a midnight excursion on which money was spent as if this were a big league in the infant class. It may be a clever trick but it is not good baseball—that's all I can say."

McCloskey's reiteration of the contemptuous term "bush" is funny, coming from him, for he seems to have found it lucrative for the last five years at least. His statment that he was forced to weaken his team is all poppycock, for the team was almost identically the same at the close of the season as it was in the beginning. McCloskey is a poor loser.

McCLOSKEY IS COMING TO PROTEST THAT GAME

The only man in Vancouver who can't see the joke, is on the warpath after Everett.

Everett Wins the Pennant

Northwest League Closes Today After A Turbulent Season

The season of the Northwest League closes today, with Everett winning the pennant. As Everett tied Vancouver for first place in the first half, and as it has been decided not to play it off, Everett will be awarded the championship after winning the second half.

It will be remembered that the Everett team was taken to Bellingham on a special train just before the close of the first half to play a postponed game at 5 o'clock in the morning. They won that game and came back to Everett to defeat Vancouver in a very exciting game in the afternoon, and thus tied for first place.

There was an awful yell from the Vancouver folks about what was called Everett Manager Hulen's sharp practice, but as everything was straight and regular there was no ground for a protest. Billy Hulen deserves a lot of credit for rounding out a winning team after getting a very bad start. Johnnie Burns helped out a lot in winning the pennant, for after he left Seattle he picked up in his hitting, and as there was never anything the matter with his fielding, second base was well taken care of.

League Had Its Troubles

The little league had its troubles as was to be expected. Victoria, with a losing team, proved to be a loser and the team was transferred to Spokane. McIntyre got some new men and he gave Everett a hot chase for the flag. He made his run just a little too late, however, to catch the flying leaders. He has proven that he can manage a team, and he will probably be retained in Spokane next year if the present circuit is maintained.

Bellingham made a runaway race of the first half of the season right up until the last two weeks. Had Manager Jack Drennan been given any money with which to get two men he would have won the pennant without question. The backers of the Bellingham team were backers in name only. They did not put up a cent before the season started nor afterward. Drennan told the writer that he had to pay the training expenses by playing exhibition games, and that the day the season opened there was not a penny in the club's treasury. Considering these conditions, the Bellingham boys made a wonderful showing, and the hand of the foxy Dugdale (who helped organize the league) was never shown to better advantage. Dug picked out that team of fast youngsters, and they made good until higher priced men in other teams put them out of it.

McCloskey was getting along all right as manager in Vancouver until he bumped into the salary limit so hard that he bounced back. He had to lop off five men at one time. They were among his highest priced men, and were his best players. His own salary suffered an awful gash and he has not been a serious factor in the second race. Vancouver comes out of the first season with one of the finest ball parks in the west, and with an appetite for baseball that will make that city a good one for any circuit next year.

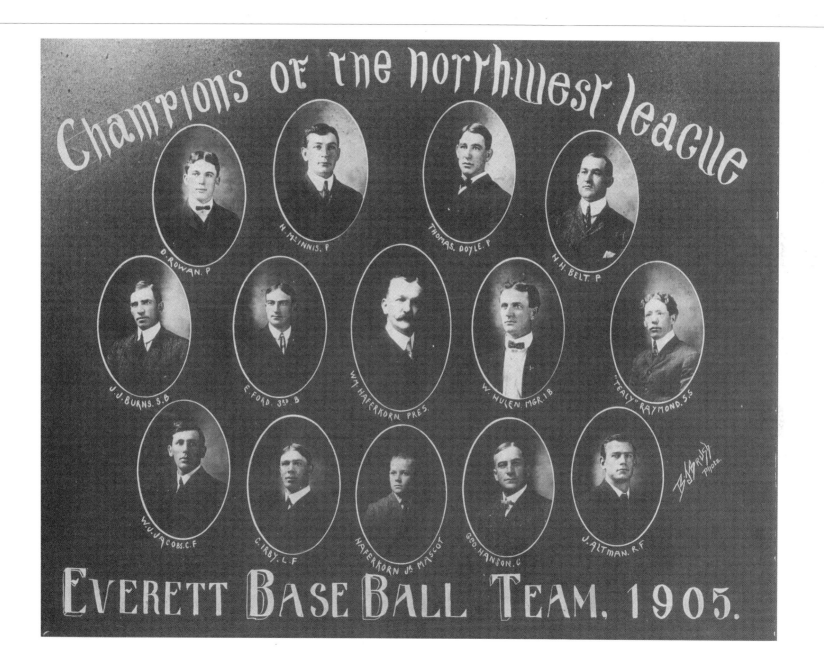

Champions of the Northwest League

EVERETT BASE BALL TEAM, 1905.

Everett Wins from Snohomish

Champions Have to Play Ball to Get the Game From the Garden City Players.

The Everett baseball team played another game at Snohomish yesterday afternoon, and again found that Snohomish played pretty good ball for amateurs. The final score was 4 to 3 in favor of the recent pennant winners of the Northwest League. The game was clean, all players being steady and doing good work with the exception of one man on the Snohomish team who handled the ball like he was scrambling eggs, and who threw at the moon and stars.

Davis of Snohomish, who plays in streaks, got a streak of the right kind and among other things worthy of commendation knocked a ball clear over the left field fence and trotted around home. Workmen in the Cascade Mill yard dodged the flying missile and thereby escaped destruction.

The most brilliant moment in the entire cloudy afternoon, was when the Snohomish fans, out of pure affection for Joe Altman, the Snohomish boy who played this year for the Everett team, presented him with a gold mounted silk umbrella with his initials engraved on the handle. Joe had no words to express thanks, but bowed low in acknowledgement of the tribute.

The game was absolutely free from kicking.

The batteries: Everett: McGinnis and Altman
Snohomish: Welch and Hoover
Umpire: Brockaw from Monroe.

Monroe, Washington, Invades Snohomish City

Baseball Fans Come Headed by Brass Band and Return With a Defeat.

Snohomish was invaded yesterday afternoon by the whole town of Monroe which marched in to the sound of music by the brass band of that city. As the mighty hosts advanced, the people of Snohomish fled in fear and trembling. Down the main street the invaders marched, across the bridge and into Harvey's park. One by one terrified citizens peered around corners, and seeing the awe inspiring procession disappearing behind the Maple Hotel, gradually regained courage and fell in behind.

It was 3:30 when time was called and Snohomish was at last face to face with the terrible willow wielders from Monroe; the stalwarts who had but one defeat against them. It looked like death by slow torture for Snohomish, not the least painful part of which would be the victorious blasts from that band of theirs.

Dead silence through the first and second innings. Then came the fatal third. Snohomish made three runs, but Monroe went them one better and got four. There were dark clouds everywhere. Snohomish tied things in the fourth, garnered three in the fifth, and allowed Monroe two more runs. Forget the rest. Snohomish got 7 in the sixth, 1 in the seventh and 3 more in the eighth. For them there was no ninth. Twice Monroe had all the bases filled, but pure, unadulterated stupidity and bum playing lost them each shining chance.

Not a drum was heard, save a funeral note, as the band moved on. It was so sad. Such patriotism, such evidence of feminine loyalty, such heaps of unshed tears! Such hordes of golden sheckels reposing snuggly in Monroe's pockets, whence the most eloquent pleadings could not draw them out for a bet. By the way, that $100 side bet never materialized.

Final score: Snohomish 18, Monroe 6.

Chapter Three: Baseball Team Pictures

List of Town Team Photos

Standing *at left wearing a bowler, Herbert H. Soule, Mayor of Anacortes.*

Back Row*, L to R: Fred Plymale, Charles Huddle, Pat Cull, Peterson.* ***Middle Row****: Clark, Mac McFarren, J.B. Riley, Jansa, Peterson.* ***Front Row:*** *Paddock, Johnnie Eagon (Mascot), Charles Barr*

Players' names on back of photo (not matched with the picture): Julian J. Hills, Geo. Elesperman Sr., Griffinn, Gus Hawkins, Lewis Monfort, Geo. Langman, Sliger, Oliver Middleton, Jim Willison, Leslie Fox, Bill Otto.

Sprouts in hats, Quicksteps in caps
Back, *L to R: Chas. Williams, Horace Holbrook, Joe Power, Will Race,_____, Howard Hill,_____,_____, Bill McCabe, Mr. Sterritt, Umpire.* **Middle**, *L to R: Arthur O'Leary, Henry Power, Harvey Crockett.* **Front**, *L to R: Fred Mowrey, Tony Monroe, Phonic Leonard, Gus Sterritt, Tibbels, Bill Van Bucklin. Port Townsend won the game, 21 to 20.*

*Left to Right:*_____, *Thomas Cain,*_____ , *Jack Cain, Dr. Jones, Patrick McCoy,*_____, *Jack Dale.*

(Spelled "EDMUNDS" on shirts, the original spelling for the town.) **Back Row**, *L to R: Enos Evans, Harold Parker, "Farmer Bill" Heberdeen, Jim Gilchrist.* **Middle Row**: *Roy Schumacher, Ernest Hubbard, "Shorty" Thurston, Frank Street.* **Front Row**: *Charley Brown, Frank Hough, Fred Saltzer.*

"Amateur Champions of the State"

Thayer and McManus

Back Row, L to R*:_____ , Noble, Molique, Frank Nevins (in tie),_____,Hollycress,_____, Klaus, Moffet.* **Seated***: Harvey, Cook, Calkins, Bockmier, Christensen, _____.* **Bat boy***: Southard*

Top Row, *from left: Charles Evans, Wylie Williams, Hugh Delanty, Ole Johnson, Billy Woodman.* **Center Row**: *Harry E. Andrson, Joe Arey, Captain Emil Larson, Wallace Bywater.* **Bottom Row**: *Alfred Van Trojen, Billy Neimier.*

Left to Right: *Charlie Philo, Bill Meurer, Moore, Robert Darnell, Harry Osgood, W.A. Fisher, Bill Fritz, Ernie Dean, Glenn Darnell, Walt Hemingway, Hagerson, Harry Gale (Mascot).*

Back Row, L to R*: Bill Starbird, Bill Hatch, storekeeper, George Starbird, Art Nelson.* **Middle Row:** *Sherman Anderson, Otis Anderson.* **Front Row:** *George Dixon, George Burns, Ted Anderson. Bat boy, Bill Swanson.*

L to R, top to bottom: Robin Welts, lf; Conner Costello, c; Rex Davison, cf; Farley Legore, Capt., p; Walter (?), utility; Walter Carr, rf; Lyle Buell, ss; Mick Martin, 2b; Phillip McCoon, manager; Floyd Gardner, lb; Gus Keppler, 3b; Red Davis, "The Jinx"

*These mill workers and loggers **dressed up** to play base ball on Sunday.*

Players' names on back of the photo (not matched with the picture): *Nat Hawkins; Frank Sullivan, Sr.; Al Jensen; Ray McLaughlin; Will Church; Willis Mathewson; Walter Dyke; Lou Gehrke; Curly Wall; Ed Shields*

Back row, L to R: Jim Blowers, Howard Graham, Sam Taylor, _____, Abe Graham, Robert Burt, Lyall Graham, Emery Raymond, Ed Blowers, Wally Bolton.
Seated, L to R: Herbie Ringenback, Phil Range, Sam Wilson Jr., Leo Towell, Claud Graham.

Front Row, L to R*: Jake Stafford, Harry Wainright, Cliff Ellis.* ***Second Row****: Harry Larson, Puget Fulk, Garnet Thompson, Lester Sharpe.* ***Third Row****: Elmer Larson, Thurston Thompson, Len Stafford, Morris Larson* ***In back****: Adam Fulk*

Photographed by Theo. E. Peiser.

BAGLEY, *1b.*   BOOTH, *c.f.*   STEVENS, *s.s.*   THORNELL, *l.f.*   KENNEY, *r.f.*   BURWELL, *c.*   JACOBS, *2b.*   BURNELL, *3b.*   DICKEY, *p.*   Second Street, near Marion, Seattle.

SEATTLE BASE BALL CLUB.

1886.

Back Row: *Shea, Weed, White, Sec'y, Seaton.* **Middle Row***: McKay, Fullerton, Dugdale, Pres., Sage, Bues, Whaling, Wigg.* **Front Row***:, Howell, Moran, Raymond, Mgr., Cruikshank, Householder, Ort, _____. (Art Bues led the Northwestern League in batting average, hits, and home runs)*

PHOTO BY LEE PICKETT

Back Row, L to R: *Rube Roberts, cf; Fred Schott, lf; Hyde Morgan, 3b; Frank Morgan, rf.* **Center Row**: *Ray Stevens, 2b & p; George Clemans, ss& mgr.; Pat Crane, utility; Ed Lysons, lb.* **Front Row**: *Percy Woodruff, mascot; Smick Meyers, p; Joe Altman, c.*

"Champions of Snohomish and Skagit Counties" Left to Right: Will Walker, Link Bucklin, Mike Sill, Dan Caldon, Charlie Bennett, Peter Harvey, William Bates, Conrad Lien. (missing from photo: Bill Caldon.)

Standing, *L to R: Hugh Eldridge, Henry Roeder Jr., William Utter, Frank Peabody, Lewis Hofercamp, William Gardner.* ***Seated****: Victor A. Roeder*

Chapter Four: Baseball Excursions

Steamboat Excursions

A favorite summer activity for the pioneers living around Puget Sound was to take an excursion on a steamer to another port town for a base ball game. In addition to the ball club, the passenger list often included the town band, the players' girl friends, parents and their wildlings, and the local newspaper editor. The Puget Sound steamers—known as "The Mosquito Fleet"— provided idyllic outings when everything went right. But sometimes things happened.

In August, 1883, the Snohomish Pacifics and some of their fans traveled to Port Gamble on the steamer *Merwin* for a base ball game which the Pacifics won 20 to 3. "The excursionists started for home at 7 o'clock in the evening, expecting to get there about midnight, but the steamer got lost in a fog off the mouth of the river. The result was that the tired and utterly disgusted party did not get home until noon the next day."

In August, 1884, the Snohomish ball club was on the way to Seattle for the second game in the championship series with the Seattle Reds when the steamer *Josephine* ran aground on a sand bar at the mouth of the Snohomish River. "The baseballists were obliged to row to Mukilteo, a distance of seven miles, in an open boat... Here they remained until the steamer *Washington* came along from Whatcom (and picked them up). When the boys arrived at the ball grounds about four o'clock they were pretty badly broken up, so to speak." Snohomish lost the game, 15 to 19.

In August, 1893, the steamer *Mabel* took the Snohomish ball club and about 75 excursionists to Port Blakely for a slugfest won by Snohomish 25 to 8. When the game was over the visiting ball tossers were given a dinner, after which the Snohomish party started home. "When about four miles below Edmonds, the *Mabel* blew out a cylinder head and one driving shaft fell overboard. After drifting about for some time the machinery was patched up and the trip home was made with only one engine. The boat arrived here (at Snohomish) at 4:30 Monday morning."

Steamer problems, of course, were not limited to trips when base ball clubs were aboard. In December, 1892, the *Snohomish Tribune* editorialized: "The racing of steamboats on the river between Snohomish and Everett is getting too frequent and should be stopped. When the rivalry between hot-headed steamboat captains reaches the pitch where the lives of passengers are endangered by racing, as was the case Monday when the *Mikado* and *Milton* were racing and collided, then it is about time that racing should cease being a virtue. If the steamboat men have a grievance let them settle it on the Sullivan-Corbett plan, as that would injure no one but themselves and that would be a small loss to the traveling public."

In April of 1899, the *Tribune* reported that at about four o'clock Sunday morning the Pacific liner *Glenogle* left the Tacoma docks in the fog and ran into the steamer *City of Kingston*, cutting her in two. The steel hull of the *Kingston* sank in seventy fathoms of water, but the upper decks floated and were towed to shore by the *Glenogle*. The officers of both vessels exerted themselves to save lives, and no passengers perished. Base ball clubs sometimes traveled on the *Kingston*, but fortuitously no players were aboard at the time of this contretemps.

Excursion to Port Gamble

Note: An example of the flowery language used at the time.

Last Sunday morning the Steamer *Nellie* got up steam and blew her first whistle at half past four o'clock. Early as it was there were plenty of lights in town, for the Pacific Base Ball Club was to try its strength against the Unknowns at Port Gamble. At half past five the boat was to start on her excursion, and those who intended to participate were already astir. After the usual delays of waiting for the last man and his Mary Jane, the final whistle was blown and we started down the river, a merry crew on pleasure bent.

About seven o'clock we reached the mouth of the river; the tide was nearly out. Bare mud flats with nothing to relieve them except a few snags, storks and gulls stretched away on our left; to the right was Priest Point; behind us were great reaches of tide marshes, and ahead Hat Island, with its great, white sand bluffs crowned with emerald. Between us and deep water was a serpentine channel, of shallow depth, whose course could be followed only by a constant use of the sounding rod. We all expected to be stuck in the mud at every revolution of the wheel, but we listened in vain for the sound of the bell. On we went, twisting and turning, heading to all points of the compass, still edging out towards Hat Island. All at once we glided into deep, blue water and were over the bar at as low a stage of water as ever a steamer had crossed before.

Many had tumbled out of bed so early—or rather so late for the boat—that they came aboard before breakfast. But no matter. We ask for no better breakfast than the one we all sat down to on board that morning. Everything was done by Capt. Low that could be done to make the trip a pleasant one.

Before we reached Gamble, the boys in blue, the Pacifics, sat down to a light lunch, preparatory to the contest to take place immediately on their arrival. We were met at the wharf by the Gamble boys, cordially welcomed and courteously entertained.

Port Gamble is a beautiful town site, and will be a beautiful town, years hence, long after the mammoth mills have become silent for want of forests to consume. It being Sunday, the mills were idle. But the presence of several large vessels at the wharves indicated the immense business of Puget Mill Company. There are several neat residences, but the chief beauty of Port Gamble is her fruit and flower gardens with which every home is ornamented. Where such evidences of taste are seen out door, there must be refinement within.

The B.B. grounds are about one mile from town. A fine road, beautifully shaded, leads out to them. The ground is not as well fitted up as it should be. There is no convenience for spectators. It is not level. The brush is too near, and the deep gulch in the rear of home base is a great draw back. This is no fault of the club. Suitable grounds are hard to be found anywhere. But, if the ground is level, all other objections can be overcome.

At fifteen minutes of twelve o'clock the game commenced with the Pacifics in the field. The game was as fair and impartial as ever was played, the only advantage being with the Unknowns who were at home and familiar with the ground. The umpire and scorers did their duty like perfect gentlemen, showing neither partiality nor favoritism. The most perfect order and decorum prevailed during the entire game. Not a word of obscene or profane language was used by either players or spectators. A great many ladies and gentlemen were present and readily expressed their approbation whenever a good play was made by either side.

The Unknowns took the lead at the start. Towards the middle of the game the Pacifics nearly caught up with them, the former being only two tallies ahead. But the Unknowns steadily gained from them till the close of the game, beating the Pacifics by a score of 38 to 22. Each club has some excellent players, but both clubs showed want of practice. Some difficult flies were skillfully taken, and many good ones missed. Much wild throwing was done on both sides, but we think the Pacifics did much more of it than their opponents. At the close of the game, rousing cheers were given for both victors

Continued on next page

and vanquished, those for the Pacifics louder than for their conquerors.

After the game, the two clubs repaired to the hotel and sat down to a magnificent banquet provided by the Unknowns. The table contained all the epicure could wish, carefully prepared and in profuse abundance. Nothing edible or drinkable was lacking. All traces of the chagrin of their defeat vanished from the faces of the Pacifics as they beheld this bountiful repast; the dinner alone was worth the trip.

The trip to Gamble and back on the *Nellie*, with the view of the heavens above, the snowy mountains with summits lost in the clouds to be seen in every direction, the mirror-like waters of our beautiful inland sea with its borders of green, reflecting the ever changing clouds, the far off mountains and the nearer foliage of evergreen forest, is worth a trip across the continent to behold. That is the way our boys felt, after parting with the Unknowns, obtaining promise from them to return the visit, shaking hands, shouting "good bye boys" as we left the wharf and waving handkerchiefs as long as anybody was in sight.

The trip home, mostly by moonlight, was a fit rounding off of a day of unalloyed pleasure. Crossing from Port Gamble to Skagit Head we had the best view of Mount Rainier we ever beheld. No matter when or from where seen, this hoary old sentinel of the ages is always grand, magnificent and sublime; but to see it as we saw it then, with the illusion of the waters of the Sound stretching far away, seemingly to the very foothills at its base, its western visage all aglow with the rays of the setting sun, will photograph a picture on the brain that life will not efface.

It was approaching midnight when we reached the wharf. We believe all hands would have gladly turned back for a repetition of the day's pleasure. We have been a five year resident of the Sound, and have never spent a happier day since we have been here.

Our Excursion

The excursion party to La Conner, although a small one, was immensely enjoyed by the victims. We made up in quality what we lacked in quantity. We landed at Lowell, Marysville and Utsalady, and gave our band a shot at the citizens as we proceeded along. We were met at La Conner by a small delegation of citizens and a "terrifyingly" abbreviated band—even more so than ours, which proceeded to walk all over theirs. After our band had aired its talent and paralyzed the natives, so to speak, we adjourned to a mud flat near by and proceeded to "do up" their pet base ball club in decidedly prompt and efficient manner, with the very able assistance of Fred Lysons of Snohomish as umpire. The score was nine to five.

After the ball game we had a "rocky time" engaging rooms, and after the usual amount of talking and scrapping that occurs when our ladies get together, we succeeded in getting accommodations after we had condensed ourselves into twos and threes in a bed. The reason that such a strain was imposed on one bed by putting three into it was that one J.V.B. ensconced himself singly and alone in a room engaged by some one else and refused to vacate it, and as it was Sunday A.M., the rightful owner of the room went her way instead of kicking up a rumpus.

The ball, which was held in the evening, was greatly enjoyed by all the participants.

Several of our young people spent Sunday forenoon in torturing livery teams and "seeing the country," delaying the departure of the steamer nearly an hour. The return trip was a pleasant one, and we arrived home early in the evening, right side up with care.

C.U. Later

Excursion to Port Gamble

Last Saturday morning the *Daisy* steamed up and at eleven o'clock blew her first whistle. At twelve, with the Dramatic Society, the base ball club, and a number of other excursionists aboard, the clipper slipped her moorings and steamed down river, enroute for Port Gamble. We counted noses and found our crowd to consist of forty-four human souls and an editor. Further on we found that this crowd, beside being talented, was possessed of considerable spirit(s) which on investigation we found to be distributed sereptitiously in long-necked demijohns, but which eventually got transferred to humanjohns with the usual results.

With a fine day, pleasant company and good music, it was impossible to have other than a pleasant trip. The music consisted of a violin, a bass viol, a cornet, and Miss Lillie Ward at the organ. At about seven o'clock we arrived at our destination and made our way to the Tekalet Hotel, where we put up—there being no other hotel to go to. After securing rooms all hands repaired to the hall where the dramatic club presented "Among the Breakers" and "Paddy Miles' Boy" to a large and appreciative audience. At the close of the entertainment a dance was announced and a large company tripped the "light fantastic" until about Sunday, probably bending the sabbath somewhately.

Those of us who did not indulge in the aforesaid fantastic retired immediately the entertainment ended. There were four of us to two single beds, a mixture rather too thick for comfort. Each of the four chose a different time for retiring, which kept things lively in our small quarters for an hour or two. When the whole party arrived, "Scud," feeling pretty happy, visited about promiscuously "in dishabille" with musical salutations until the shower bath act quieted things down. That pitcher of "aqua chuck" dampened Mr. Scud's snowy raiment just below that part of his physical anatomy known as the small of the back. There was an "O-O-O! Oh!" and a flap and a bang, and then silence, broken only by some haw-hawing as the dampened "Scud" crawled into the straw for a long refreshing sleep.

Sunday morning the "Snohomish Pacifics" and the "Port Gamble Unknowns" were on the ground at 9:30. At 10 time was called and the game opened. The first inning was a close one and stood one to one, but starting in the second the Unknowns showed their lack of practice. To make matters worse, some of their old members who usually do good work played badly out of luck. For the Pacifics, Moore scored only one run, but his teammates each crossed home plate at least three times. The final score was Pacifics 31, Unknowns 11.

After the game, which lasted until 12:30, the Unknowns gave the usual dinner with right good will, even if they did get beat, and kept up their reputation for being "jolly good fellows."

About 2PM the crowd once more boarded ship, the music struck up, goodbyes were hastily said, and compliments exchanged. The *Daisy* moved slowly away homeward bound, arriving at Snohomish about 10 o'clock after a very pleasant trip. Even the tuneful "Scud" turned up smiling and sober—the next morning.

The dampened Scud crawled into the straw for a long sleep

Excursion on the *George E. Starr*

Snohomish Outing Enjoyed By All.

Balmy Breezes, Band Music, Courteous Treatment and Baseball Victory Make Excursion a Grand Success.

The excursion to Fort Worden yesterday could not possibly have been a greater success. The steamer *George E. Starr* was comfortably filled, and all day long the excursionists enjoyed pleasant weather, excellent treatment, good music, and the very best of good times.

Leaving the Everett Improvement Company's dock at 8:45a.m., the whistle sounded and the boat steamed across Puget Sound for Fort Worden, where the ball game with the soldiers was played on the beautiful parade grounds.

Snohomish went into the game somewhat handicapped by the fact that Right Fielder Morgan has a broken collar bone and could not play, and that Backstop Hoover did not accompany the team. Ed Lysons caught, and for two or three innings could not master Pitcher Whitfield's curves, but in a little while he settled down to work and Snohomish played winning ball from that time on.

Lieutenant Olmstad umpired the game and at times erred somewhat, but it did no good for Snohomish to kick, and the soldier lads did not dare to do so.

Snohomish made one run in the first, and Worden got two. Snohomish then pulled down five goose-eggs; so did Worden. In the seventh, the first Snohomish batter fanned. Then two men got on bases, another fanned, and little Kelso, the youngster who was playing in Morgan's position, came to bat. Snohomish fans groaned, for the lad was sized up by his years and not by his prowess as a hitter. He smote the air twice, and while he was doing this one man got to third and the other to second. Everyone held his breath. The bat cut the air with a vicious swish and the ball was knocked far afield. Kelso reached second and two men came home. Pitcher Thomas for Worden got rattled and the Snohomish boys got two more runs before the inning ended.

In the ninth Snohomish bunched their hits and two more tallies were made. The final score was 7 to 3.

Although few of the excursionists were aware of the fact, they had the unique experience of seeing a convict play ball. Some of the soldiers told that one of the players was taken out of the guard house, where he awaits sentencing as a convicted deserter, just for the purpose of playing ball. He will probably not enjoy another game until a sentence of two years is served in a federal prison. A sentinel, gun in hand, patrolled the grounds, probably for the purpose of seeing that the player did not escape, rather than keeping Snohomish from mobbing the umpire.

Northwest Steamships

These steamers were among many used for Baseball Excursions.

NAME	TYPE	YEAR BUILT	LENGTH	BEAM	HOLD
NELLIE	Sternwheeler	1876	80'	19'4"	4'9"
GEORGE E. STARR	Sidewheeler	1878-9	144' *	28'	9'
ROSALIE	Hybrid sail & steam (propeller)	1893	136'	27'	10'
CITY of EVERETT	Propeller	1900	134'	21'	6'7"

* One source lists the Starr as 154' long.

 The early settlements in the Pacific Northwest were along waterways, and transportation between towns was by boat. On Puget Sound these boats were called the "Mosquito Fleet" and there were dozens of them. From 1864 to 1904 there were over 60 different steamships that called at the town of Snohomish on the Snohomish River. These ships were owned by many different private companies who were in fierce competition for passengers and freight. They raced each other from port to port, and mishaps were inevitable.

Historical Tidbits About the Steamships Pictured

NELLIE —A shallow draft sternwheeler that could go a long way up the rivers, even during seasons of low water. She was the first steamer on a regularly scheduled run between Seattle and Snohomish.

GEORGE E. STARR—She was considered fast when she was launched in 1879. She made remarkable voyages to Skagway during the Klondike gold rush. Eventually the infirmities of age slowed her down so much that she inspired the oft repeated ditty:

"Paddle, paddle *George E. Starr,*
How we wonder where you are.
Left Seattle at half past ten,
Gets to Bellingham, God knows when."

The *Starr* became not only slow, but crotchety. When making turns she would often list over and fail to right herself, thus lifting one sidewheel out of the water, causing her to limp around in circles until enough weight could be shifted to the high side to stabilize her.

By 1911 the historic old vessel was tied up to a buoy in the Seattle harbor, where she was used to store powder and explosives which could not be brought in to the docks at night. Not long after she was moved to Lake Union for dismantling.

ROSALIE — Her primary propulsion was by a steam driven propeller with an assist from her sails when the winds were favorable. She was built in Alameda in 1893 and sent north to Puget Sound. During the Klondike gold rush she was put on the run to Alaskan ports. After the gold fever subsided she returned to the Seattle/ Port Townsend/ Victoria run. On June 22, 1918, the venerable old steamer was destroyed by fire while laid up in the West Waterway, Seattle.

CITY OF EVERETT—Was built in Everett in 1900 at the Sumner Iron Works. She was a fast boat and her captain delighted in racing other boats. *The Seattle Times* reported that when on the Bellingham route she ran into the Steamer *Kitsap* twice within a few days. There was no major damage, but the maritime officials considered the captain sufficiently at fault to suspend his license for thirty days.

Upon her retirement from sea duty she was used as the Ballard Yacht Club. In the 1960's she was used as a floating restaurant on Seattle's Lake Union. There the proud ship sank in shallow water, was raised again, sank again, and gradually disintegrated.

Steamer *Nellie,* ca 1877

Steamer *George E. Starr*

Steamer *Rosalie*

Demise of the *Rosalie* • *June 22, 1918*

Steamer *City of Everett*

Chapter Five: Native American Baseball

Native American (Indian) Athletics

The North American Indians have a tradition going back uncounted generations of playing games involving the hitting of a moving ball with a stick or racket. In addition to lacrosse, the tribes across the United States played a game called "shinny." This was a rough game played mostly by men, although in some tribes it was also played by women. There were few rules other than some basics. In their 1930 book "THE INDIANS OF PUGET SOUND," ethnologists Haeberlin and Gunther reported that "shinny was played in the summertime on the beach or prairie. It was always an intertribal contest, with slaves, canoes, shells, or blankets as stakes. Each tribe selected twelve to twenty of its best men and a captain. The men were naked except for a breechclout. Each man had two sticks curved on one end. With the stick in his left hand he defended himself. The ball was of cedar or fir wood, a little larger than a baseball. The object of the game was to drive the ball across the adversary's goal at the end of a field from two hundred yards to a mile long. The ball was started in the center. Pushing a player aside or tripping him on one's stick was permissable. To win, one side had to put the ball over the goal line twice in succession."

When baseball was introduced, the Indians had already developed the hand-eye coordination necessary to hit a pitched ball with a bat. Many pictures of early town teams include one or more Indians. The reservations had their own teams which played each other and also many non-native teams. There is a newspaper reference to a baseball team on the Tulalip Reservation (Snohomish County, Washington) in 1884. This initial advantage of the Indians was eventually lost as all kids in the next generation grew up playing baseball.

The next impetus for Indian baseball came with the establishment of Indian boarding schools starting in the late 1800's. There was a Federal Boarding School for both boys and girls on the Tulalip Reservation from 1905 to 1932. Children from tribes other than the Tulalips were removed from their homes and enrolled at the Tulalip school. From the standpoint of Indian culture, the Federal Boarding Schools were a disaster. One of the few bright spots in the boarding school system was organized athletics for both boys and girls. The kids were taught the rules of games, were given coaching in the skills necessary to play the games well, were provided with equipment and uniforms, and were allotted times for practice and for competitions. With their natural aptitude and some coaching, the Indians learned to play their opponents even, and if the officiating was reasonably fair, would often win.

Athletic events were one of the few opportunities the boarding school students had for socializing. The boys and girls were otherwise separated, but could mingle as spectators at sporting events. Additionally, their teams became a source of great pride to them as Indians, which was contrary to the administrators' goal of assimilation.

The most prominent of the boarding schools was Carlisle Indian School in Pennsylvania. The success of their football teams is legendary, but they also had outstanding baseball players. Seven former Carlisle students played in the Major Leagues, and one, Charles A. "Chief" Bender, is enshrined in the National Baseball Hall of Fame.

Among the Northwest tribes, baseball was the dominant team sport. The most distinguished Indian athlete from the area, however, was a football player, Thomas Yarr of the Snohomish tribe. He was the center on the national champion Notre Dame football team in 1930. He was the team captain in 1931, and was named to the Associated Press All-American team. In 1982 he was honored by being inducted into the American Indian Athletic Hall of Fame, and in 1987 was inducted into the College Football Hall of Fame.

With the passage of time, the closing of Indian boarding schools, and intermarriage, there are now fewer prominent athletes identified as "Indian." At the same time, there is an increasing emphasis on education, and Indians are more and more distinguishing themselves in fields other than athletics.

THE SEATTLE POST-INTELLIGENCER • SEATTLE, WASHINGTON • JULY 19, 1894

Baseball on Saturday

Port Townsend Athletic Club Will Be The Attraction

The team which will represent Port Townsend here will be one of the strongest combinations to play at Madison Park this season. The Seattle Athletic Club beat them last month only after a hard fight, the score standing 6 to 5. Their pitcher, Wood, is a full-blooded Indian, who stands close on to seven feet in height. He has tremendous speed, and in the Port Townsend game the Seattle batsmen did not hit him hard. A short time before the game he had rowed eighteen miles to be there for the match and so was not at his best. Since then he has had considerable experience, which will be of great benefit to him, as this is his first season of pitching.

Back Row, *L to R:* _____, *Clement Bob, William Shelton (holding pennant), Robert Shelton (William's son), Roy Loughrey, Joseph Joe.*
Seated on right: *Augustus Day. The other players are not identified.*

Indians Not in the Expert Class

Everett Held the Visitors to a Single Run.

Thornton's Stick Work Showed the Effects of Two Weeks at the Fishpole.

The Chemawa Indians (from Oregon) met their Waterloo against Everett's prize aggregation yesterday afternoon. They went down by a score of 13 to 1 which would indicate mighty poor ball to the average fan, but all around it wasn't slow. The red men were simply outclassed, but to their credit it must be said they put up fairly good ball. Their pitcher, Graham, did some fairly clever work, but wasn't in it a little bit with McKay of Everett, who pitched an exceptionally good game. With a solitary exception Everett played an errorless game. One of the main features was the heavy batting of Donovan, Bird and James, of the locals. Thornton, Everett's star first baseman, however, contrary to precedent, made three ineffective attempts to connect with the sphere. This is attributed to the enervating effects of camp life. Game summary:

Earned runs: Everett 6, Chemawa 1. Hits: Everett 17, Chemawa 4.

Left on base: Everett 7, Chemawa 4. Struck out: by McKay 10, by Graham 4. Wild pitches: Graham 1.

Umpire: Wingate.

Time of game: 1:25.

Everett Team is Defeated

Tulalip Baseballists Prove Themselves Too Strong

The red men yesterday demonstrated that there are times when his white brother isn't in it. Yesterday, as far as baseball was concerned, was one of those times. An Everett team met the Tulalip team at the reservation and went down to ignominious defeat. The score was 16 to 2 in favor of the reservation people.

The game took place Sunday afternoon as one of the events of the Odd Fellows' picnic to Tulalip, and it proved a feature of the day. The Everett team was composed of many of the best players in Everett, but they found that they could do nothing with the Indian aggregation.

Yesterday's picnic was even more successful than the one given on the Fourth. The steamer *Ellwood* was kept busy carrying people back and forth all day, and the last picnickers were not brought home until late at night. It is estimated that there were about 1,500 people at Tulalip Sunday, and 1,100 Saturday. Both crowds were very orderly, and had a first class time.

A feature of yesterday's sports was several Indian canoe races.

Standing, L to R: *Levi Lamont, clerk, _____ , Jim Scott.* **Keeling**: *Alec Bagley, Bill Day (Bill Shelton's brother).* **Sitting**: *Robert Shelton, Joseph Joe, George Jones (Stan Jones' father), Joe Dunbar.*

Indians Play a Ten Inning Game

Everett Team Wins Out By Only One Score

Indians Knock Two Pitchers Out of the Box, and Start on a Third

The Clark-Nickerson team of Everett managed to defeat the Tulalip Indians on the diamond last night, but they did it by only one score, and it required ten innings at that. It was the first ten inning game of the season.

Some of the members of the Indian team have the making of good ball players. Peter Sam does well behind the bat, and Cy Hatch gaffles on to most everything that comes along at second. Percival, at third, can't throw, but he is pretty sure in holding the ball when it is thrown to him.

The Indians batted two of Everett's pitchers out of the box, and did a few things to a third. Foran started in to throw for Everett, and then Grace was substituted. But he did not make good, and Parker, of the papermill crowd, finished the game.

The game was tied in the eighth inning, at twelve scores each, and both sides were shut out in the ninth. And then pandemonium broke loose. When the tenth began, the Indians put on their war paint and got out their scalping knives, but it was of no avail. They could not get a man past second. The locals got a man in in their half and the game was over.

The lineup for the Tulalips:

Sam,

Percival,

A. Hatch,

James,

Cy Hatch,

Jones,

Henry,

Dunbar,

Williams,

MARYSVILLE GLOBE • JUNE 1905

Indian Meets Indian

JUNE 2: What promises to be an event in the local baseball world this season is the series of games between the Lummi Indians and the Tulalips. The Lummi team is composed of big fellows. The teams have never met before. Neither team has met defeat in any of the games played with other teams. They are the strongest Indian teams in this part of the country. The lineup for Tulalip will be as follows:

Peter Sam, George Wykes, James Scott, Andrew Fryberg, Arthur Hatch, Cy Hatch, Ezra Hatch, Emil Williams, Ed Percival.

The games will be played in the Marysville baseball park. It is hoped that Marysville will turn out in full force and root for Tulalip, as well as make these games successful. Admission is 25 cents as usual.

Lummis vs. Tulalips

June 9: It is seldom that Tulalip is so well represented in town as it was last Sunday. It seemed as if the whole reservation must have come to town. Front Street was full of people. The occasion was the games between the Lummi and Tulalip baseball teams.

A series of three games had been advertised, one to be played Saturday afternoon and two on Sunday. On account of heavy rain, the Saturday game was omitted. In the Sunday morning game the Tulalips won by a score of 13 to 12. In the afternoon the Lummis braced up and took the game by a score of 6 to 5. Special interest attached to the games because it was the first time the teams had met, and neither team had met defeat. In the games of last Sunday both met defeat, but neither team has established its superiority, so a return series will probably be played with Lummi on their home grounds.

Left to Right, prone or sitting: Al Charles,_____, Herman McClosky, Ed McClosky, Walter James,_____, _____, _____, Tommy Tom, Art Kwina. **Standing**: Art Kittles.

Chapter Six: Umpires

BELLINGHAM BAY MAIL.

The Tribune-Review

Devoted to the interests of Edmonds-On-The Sound---"The City of Opportunity"

The Stanwood Press.

VOL. 3. STANWOOD, WASHINGTON, SATURDAY, AUG. 20, 1898

Umpires

"A Policeman's Lot Is Not A Happy One, Happy One."
GILBERT AND SULLIVAN

Were it ever thus.

In pioneering days each baseball team had its own umpire. He could be a former player. Sometimes it was one of a team's own players who might be injured or for some reason was not playing. They used only one umpire who stood behind the pitcher and called balls and strikes, plays on the bases, and foul balls down the line. The first pitch of the game would be preceded by a prolonged argument to determine who's umpire was going to work the game. Only one game was noted where the two teams agreed to alternate umpires each inning.

There were no schools for umpires in those days. Written rules, if available, were rudimentary. Arguments were won by the team shouting the loudest. Decisions were changed based on intimidation.

Umpires were known to bet on the games they were officiating. The umpires themselves took plenty of abuse, from being roughed up by players to being pelted by rotten eggs and fruit on their way out of town.

The early players must have loved playing baseball and accepted the adversarial role with the umpire as part of the game.

Knocks With Hammer

Delivered With the Hope of Doing the Game No Harm

Good Umpires Are Hard to Get
An Occasional Error Should be Overlooked.

To begin, it may truthfully be remarked that there isn't enough money in the world to hire the average man who knows anything about baseball as she is played to act as an umpire in a league game. It is a trying position; and the fact that so few people make any allowances for its difficulty makes it all the more trying. This is not meant to convey the impression that players have no rights which an umpire is bound to respect. Simply a reminder that change does not always mean improvement in umpires. There may be three or four ideal umpires in the busines; they are in the employ of the National and American leagues.

Yesterday, to bring the matter to its local application, King, the Bellingham rightfielder, was ordered off the field and off the grounds for talking back to Umpire Derrick. No one in the grandstand heard what the local player said to Derrick, and the first they knew of the incident was when King was being chased over the fence to the clubhouse.

Probably the umpire's action was arbitrary and unnecessarily severe. But it is doubtful if anything will be gained by attempting a change, which certain officers of the local club say they are contemplating. Derrick's work has, on the whole, been the best seen here this season; and it hardly seems a safe precedent to set, to discharge men for being over severe—the opposite fault might be worse, and, as stated before, most of the ideal umpires have good jobs in the big leagues.

Yesterday's Game Won by the Home Team

**If All the Players Could Bat as Hard as They Can Kick,
the Fence Around Pastime Park Would Never Stop the Ball.**

The game of ball at Pastime Park yesterday between Snohomish and Stanwood was what the cranks would call rocky. Besides loose playing there was a continuous kick from start to finish. Billy Booth umpired the game, and it was his decisions that made the trouble.

Snohomish started off at its usual canter and made five runs in the first inning. A little later came the first grand kick. Caldon, shortstop for Stanwood, was touched by Roll between second and third. The umpire called the runner out, although Roll dropped the ball. For a minute there was pandemonium. Bob Hulbert swore he would play no more, but thought better of it. The game had just started up again when another rumpus occurred. This time Raynor of Snohomish was touched just as he slid over the home plate. He was safe enough, but to even things up the umpire called him out.

The game proceeded. It was about the fourth inning. Raynor struck three times. The third was a passed ball, and there being no one on base he started to run. "Batter out!" said the umpire. Roll let out a yell of protest that made the welkin ring, and jumped stiff legged. He also drew the base ball statutes on the umpire and demanded a hearing. It wouldn't go and Roll jumped the game.

The kicking diminished in vigor from this time forward. On one occasion Captain Thornton had to rebuke the Stanwood pitcher for hitting so many men, but it did not delay the game.

Up to the end of the seventh inning Stanwood had only two runs, while Snohomish had fifteen. Then the visitors knocked a hole through the Snohomish battery and in the eighth scored six times amid the wildest excitement. Snohomish took the cue and added four marks in the eighth and one in the ninth, the game ending as follows: Snohomish 20, Stanwood 8.

Putrified Umpiring

The New Base Ball Maxim:
"Let Us Have Our Umpire and We Care Not Who Has the Battery."

It is fortunate for the success of base ball in Snohomish this season that the system of rotten umpiring inaugurated within the past month was not introduced earlier. Nearly all the visiting clubs have brought their umpire with them, and as a result the home team has had the worst of the decisions all summer. Superior playing, however, has placed the whole series of games to the credit of Snohomish, which suffered its first defeat at the hands of an aggregation of professionals calling themselves the Teamsters of Seattle. The first time that club came here this season it was beaten out of sight. The members were not discouraged, however, and came again, it being understood that they had greatly strengthened their team. Before the game had progressed very far the people of Snohomish understood what was meant by strengthening a team. It consists in adding a tenth man, and having that man umpire the game.

The same thing happened last Sunday when Port Gamble came to play its second game, after having been once defeated. Lumsden, better known as "Slivers," who pitched last year for Gamble, was Sunday's umpire. His appointment appears to have been arranged beforehand without consultation with Captain Oliver Thornton. The audience called for Morath, and Thornton asked him to serve, but Slivers had already got out of his coat and into the diamond. He took his station behind Gamble pitcher Horton, and never moved from that place throughout the game. His decisions on balls were errors, on strikes they were crimes, on fouls they were outrages, and at the bases they were sins against the Holy Ghost!

The Snohomish players bore patiently with him until a foul tip landed the ball near the race track behind the players' bench. Slivers called it a strike and the Gamble runners moved two bases ahead, although everybody on the grounds had heard the bat and the ball collide. Of course there was a protest, but the decision stood. Within five minutes Wilson of the Gambles tried to slide to second, but stuck in the mud a yard from the base and Roll touched him out. The umpire said "Safe!" It was enough to make an admirer of clean ball faint away. All the infield protested. The Gamble boys hugged themselves and turned their faces away from the scene. Roll registered a vehement kick. Thornton objected. The spectators hissed and would have endorsed the home team if they had thrown up the game then and there. But it went on, the visitors gaining two runs by that piece of infamy. There was not an inning unmarked by similar incidents. Oliver Thornton was called out at third even though McInnes failed to hold the ball after touching him. Horton bunted a little one to the ground, six feet in front of him, and then threw his bat at it, sending the ball to the middle of the diamond, just as Bird was about to pick it up and throw him out. The score stood about even and it was anyone's game barring Slivers, but the audience was disgusted and showed its disapprobation by going away. When the last inning closed, with the score Port Gamble 9, Snohomish 4, the grand stand was empty.

The juveniles did not allow Slivers to depart without paying him their respects, and at the boat they treated him to several volleys of decayed fruit, watermelons, and bad eggs, some of which were aimed with sufficient accuracy to leave their mark upon his person. It was the first time in history that this distinction has been accorded an umpire here, and shows that there is a point beyond which forbearance does not apply.

The umpire was treated to several volleys of decayed fruit and rotten eggs

Tacoma-Everett Ball Game

Yesterday's baseball game at Tacoma between the Tacoma Athletic Club and the Everett team was forfeited to Tacoma by a score of 9 to 0 on a decision of Umpire Chubb with Everett at bat in the eighth inning.

With one man out and Roberts on third, Bird had hit to Peer, the Tacoma pitcher, and he threw home to shut out Roberts, who had started for the plate. McLean and Harkens then "ran down" Roberts, Bird in the meantime stealing second and third. Everett raised some point, and while the two teams were wrangling over it and the umpire was calling "play ball," Bird was caught napping off third base, at least so the Tacoma team claimed.

Umpire Chubb first stated that he did not see the play, but when pressed for a decision declared Bird out. Then Everett "kicked" in earnest. They declared they would not proceed with the game unless the decision was reversed or another umpire substituted, so Umpire Chubb declared the game forfeited to Tacoma. (At that time the score stood 12 to 10 in Tacoma's favor.)

When the decision was made known the "rooters" left the bleachers and gathered around the opposing teams demanding that Tacoma yield the point to Everett and let the game proceed, but Umpire Chubb declared that his decision had been given and it must stand, and Tacoma stood with him.

Mr. Chubb is a professional ball player who arrived in the city yesterday, and he was asked to umpire the game, under the impression that he would be satisfactory to both teams. However, Chubb's decisions throughout the game were shaky, and created no little dissatisfaction in the grand stand. He was generally partial to the home team.

Peer was pitching his best ball when the game was called and it is doubtful if the result would have been changed. The features of the game were the heavy batting, the rank decisions of the umpire and all the fielding errors.

How it Happened

Vancouver Umpire Stole the First Game

The Everett ball team returned last night from its eventful trip to Vancouver, B.C. In a nut shell the full story of their defeat at the Britishers' hands is as follows: Upon arriving in Vancouver Captain Thornton was warned by the better element of baseball rooters not to play, as the Vancouver umpire had openly advised bets placed on the Vancouver team, saying at the same time he would see that his men won.

The Everett team was behind some $90 for expenses and said they would play notwithstanding the unfavorable aspect of things.

The umpire carried out his threat to the letter, many of his decisions being so ludicrously unfair as to disgust Vancouver people, who again approached Captain Thornton suggesting the name of an honest man and a gentleman to umpire the second game of the series. The Vancouver team objected strongly to this change in umpires, but Thornton told them an honest man would umpire the second game or Everett would not play.

And so the game was played and Everett this time was defeated fairly and by superior playing. Pitcher George Clemens occupied the box for Everett in this second game, Schoch being ill during the trip.

Umpire Was Too Strong for Everett's Aggregation

He Outplayed 'Em At Every Point With His Unique Curved Decisions

Speaking of Sunday's Seattle League team vs Everett game, the *Post Intelligencer* patriotically remarked that Pitcher Stovall "had big Walter Thornton guessing." Thornton claims that it was Umpire Harmon who had him guessing, and Everett fans who saw the games say both Saturday and Sunday matches were umpired by Seattle players and umpired most unfairly. The game Sunday was not especially interesting though it resulted in a Na-tional League score and was close throughout. The attendance was 2500.

Everett took the field, Schoch occupying the box. The new player, Shanweber, held down second and played good ball. Schoch, who put up a strong game, only gave three men a base on balls.

Everett had Seattle going in the ninth inning but couldn't make good. In this inning Pringle was hit by Stovall and took second on a fast single to right made by LeBeau. Thornton sent a slow one, Pringle taking third and Thornton reached first safely, though LeBeau died on second. Thornton stole second but Pringle proved himself too cagy to try to come home. Schmidt smashed out a good one, but unfortunately it was muzzled and Pringle failed to score, though he made a hard slide to get in under the ball. There was a howl of anguish and rage from the Everett contingent at this de-cision, for they claimed Pringle was safe. Schmidt was snowed under trying to steal second and the game was over.

	1	2	3	4	5	6	7	8	9	R	H	E
EVERETT	0	0	0	0	0	0	0	0	0—	0	3	0
SEATTLE	1	0	1	0	0	0	0	0	0—	2	2	3

Snohomish Loses in a Hard Game

Umpires Gave Everett The Best Of It

Heitmuller is Taken Out of the Box
to Give Smokestackers a Chance to Win

If ever a whirlwind of excitement struck a grand stand at a ball game, that twister gambolled across Harvey Park in Snohomish yesterday afternoon, when the giants of Everett came up to make monkeys out of the poor little amateurs. It was whoop and yell all through. The champions pranced onto the diamond with smiles of confidence on their faces and with the intention of playing easy and letting Snohomish make almost as many scores as they; but, alas, they were surprised! The Snohomish team convinced them in less than two innings that there was material up their way, and that Snohomish knew a few things about ball.

The umpire was Irby, of Spokane, and his work was so rank that the grand stand demanded his removal. He went, and Billy Hart of Snohomish took his place. Billy erred also, but his mistakes must have been honest ones, as they cost Snohomish the game, unless every Snohomish fan in town is mistaken.

Judgens on second hit a streak of bad luck, including being knocked over by one of the burly fellows from Everett, but in spite of his errors Snohomish won that match.

With two Snohomish men on bases, a fair ball was knocked by Morgan near the foul line out in right. Hart called it a foul, and the two base runners who came home were ordered back on bases and the batter called back from first. As one of these runners afterwards got home, this ruling cost Snohomish one run.

Again, with the bases full, Heitmuller blocked a runner and two more men came home. But back they went on bases upon the umpire's orders.

From the very beginning of the game until the end of the eighth, Snohomish played fast ball. So did Everett, with the possible exception of the few seconds it took the Smokestackers to get over their foolish dream at the beginning of the game. Any talk to the effect that they fooled along till the ninth is ridiculous. They had to play ball to stay in the game. In the ninth, things came their way and they piled five runs on top of their solitary score, making them six and giving them just one run the best of it. The bad decisions set aside, as they surely should have been, would have given the game to Snohomish by a margin of two runs, the final score would then have been 8 to 6 instead of 5 to 6.

Heitmuller was put in the box to toy with the Snohomish batters, but in the sixth he was retired and Doyle, one of the magic twirlers, rushed to the rescue. Snohomish found him, just as they did the Dutchman, and it was not his fault Everett won out. The Smokestackers did not make a single earned run.

	R	H	E
Everett	6	4	4
Snohomish	5	8	6

Batteries: Everett-Heitmuller, Doyle and Altman;

Snohomish-Williamson and Hoover.

Rotten Eggs for Stanwood Umpire

Umpire Ruth, a Stanwood Man, is Forced Off Diamond by Snohomish Players

The amateur league game played at Snohomish yesterday between Stanwood and Snohomish, broke up in a row in the ninth inning, after as pretty a game as ever was played on the home grounds. The score stood 3 to 3 in the top of the ninth when the Snohomish boys insisted that Umpire Ruth, who had persistently given rank decisions against Snohomish, should make way for another man. Stanwood would not stand for the change and walked off. In the general confusion that followed, Ruth declared the game forfeited to Stanwood by a score of 9 to 0. In the meantime Umpire Smith had been called on the grounds, Snohomish had taken positions, and after duly calling time, Smith declared the game forfeited to Snohomish by a score of 9 to 0.

For eight innings Stanwood had had their own umpire, for owing to the resignation of the regularly appointed league umpire after a disgraceful disagreement at Stanwood a week ago, the Stanwood Director had taken it upon himself to appoint Ruth, who had until now been Stanwood's center fielder, to umpire the game. Snohomish is unanimously of the opinion that as an umpire Ruth is the most polished and artistic robber that ever waved a pinion over the local field.

Ruth gave Snohomish the worst of it on balls and strikes all through the game—invariably at critical times—and to throw off suspicion, once in a while rendered wrong decisions against Stanwood, but never when they counted for anything.

As an indication of where the umpire's preferences lay it is only necessary to quote Shortstop Davis and Second Baseman Kelso, who heard him say to a Stanwood base runner, "Slide, slide!"

Manager Lysons for Snohomish, said in regard to the muddle: "Snohomish acted within her rights. It was understood when the league was organized, that if an umpire gave decisions that were absolutely distasteful to one or both of the nines, that a protest could be made and the umpire fired off the field. We stood Ruth's rotten work for eight innings, but when he started in to rob us again in the ninth, then we insisted on his vacating. After we ordered him, or rather, forced him from the field, he had no authority whatever, and his decision against us was of no force or effect."

Mr. Lysons refers to a decision in the ninth when as pretty a strike as ever went over the plate was called a ball, at a time when Stanwood had a man on second and no one out.

The gate receipts are still in the possession of Treasurer J.L. Lysons, and will remain in his possession pending an adjustment of the dispute. The game will be protested and settled by the league board. The game was to be for a division of the gate receipts, 60 per cent to the winner. The Stanwood boys say they received nothing.

The report from Stanwood in *The Seattle Post-Intelligencer* that rotten eggs were thrown at their team when it left town, has been found to be correct, but the offense has been traced to a lot of irresponsible young kids. The eggs were thrown at the umpire, outside the city limits, on the way to the Great Northern depot, but fell short of their mark. Until the P-I got here this morning, the city officials did not know anything about it. It is probable that arrests will follow. The people here regret the incident as much as the Stanwood people resent it.

Electrics May Quit league

Manager Cotterill Claims Umpire Bird Gave a Wrong Decision at Monroe Sunday Which Cost His Team the Game

Manager Cotterill of the Seattle Electrics submits the following case to the sporting editor of The Times for settlement:

"The pitcher delivered a wide ball to the batter who to avoid being hit stepped back out of the box, the ball striking his bat. Does this not count as a strike, there being at that time only one strike on the batter?

"At Monroe last Sunday in the last half of the ninth inning with the score 7 to 6 in favor of the Electrics, the Monroe team had a man on first and second bases with two out. Umpire Bird got bad then and called everything a ball unless the batter swung at it. The batter having swung once, fouled the next one, but the umpire ruled that it counted as nothing as the batter had stepped out of the box. As the latter swung on the next one in vain he would have been out had the foul referred to been called a strike, and the side retired, giving the game to the Electrics. As it was the batter drew a base on balls and the next man up drove in the winning runs.

"The Electrics believe the umpire was in error, and if he was, the game certainly belonged to the Electrics and if their position is correct, and the game is not awarded to them, the Electrics intend to withdraw from the Western Washington Amateur League."

If Manager Cotterill states the case correctly, Umpire Bird was clearly in the wrong. Every ball pitched must be called something by the umpire. If it was a foul tip, when there was only one strike on the hitter, then it counts for a strike. It does not matter in the least that the batter was ducking away from the ball when it struck his bat. His awkwardness in getting away does not help him any in this case. It looks as if the manager of the Electrics had a good kick coming and some action should be taken by the officials. He would be foolish to withdraw from the league if he is not awarded the game, however, for the sporting world hates a quitter.

Double Umpire System Not Working Out Well

The double-umpire system, which was originated for the purpose of assuring the players an unusual safeguard against inability of the arbiters to see the true merits of close plays, does not seem to be working in a manner entirely beyond reproach.

In spite of the system of double-umpiring which has been used almost exclusively this season in the Major Leagues, there have been many justly-founded complaints against the arbiters' decisions that have been made this year. Fully half of them have been made in games where there have been two men to watch the plays. This, of course, may be blamed to some extent on the individuality of the umpires, but it seems that a more even distribution or a particular rule would make both umpires more useful in defining very close plays.

The only mention in the Rule Book of the divided functions of two umpires in the same game is Rule 74, which reads as follows: "If two umpires be assigned to a game the assistant umpire shall decide all plays at first and second bases." If this is taken as closely bounding the function of the second umpire, he does not have enough to do. Two out of three times he can see what goes on at third base and what occurs in the outfield—for instance, whether an outfielder catches a low fly before it strikes the ground or not much more plainly than the head arbiter behind home plate.

Chapter Seven: Challenge Matches

Challenge Matches

Challenge Matches were a widely popular form of summer entertainment from the late 1800's to the First World War. (Challenge Matches continued to be played after that time, but other diversions captured spectator interest.)

A group of men would challenge another group to a game of baseball with the proceeds from the sale of tickets and refreshments going to a local charity such as the public library, hospital or fire company.

Matches were played by ad hoc teams assembled for that event; e.g.:
- Bankers vs. Lawyers
- Bayside vs. Riverside
- Married Men vs. Bachelors
- Fats vs. Leans
- Jr. Law Students vs. Sr. Law Students

Sportswriters' imaginations were at their most inventive in reporting the games. Scurrilous barbs were hurled back and forth in the local newspapers for days before the games.

Outrageous costumes were the uniform of the day. Blatantly biased rule changes were proposed by each team.

Substitutions were frequent, and any affiliated man willing to play the fool could get in the game. A brass band would march in to add to the clangorous noise from the cowbell orchestra seated in the top row of the grandstand.

There was no Mercy Rule. In October, 1895, the Snohomish Printers were whipping the Barbers 136 to 4 at the end of the second inning. The Barbers then threw in the towel. The losing group would often demand a rematch. More fun and more money for charity.

Baseball was the National Game, and every community, large or small, had its Town Team. Participation in the Town Team, however, was reserved for the gifted athletes, many of whom were recruited from out-of-town. Competition was intense.

Challenge Matches, by contrast, were strictly local with the objective of having fun for both the players and fans (cranks). Players were "good sports" rather than skilled. It was very humanizing for the townsfolk to see their doctor/banker/lawyer in a clown costume. People left the ball grounds in a holiday mood, satisfied that justice had triumphed and that charity had been served.

Money Power Triumphant

Cunning of Attorneys Availeth Nothing

BANKERS 22, LAWYERS 14

In this city yesterday afternoon the money power triumphed again. Local Bankers marched on the diamond decked in gala attire, wearing silk shirts and costumes gaudier than Joseph's famous coat of many colors, arrogantly flaunting in the faces of their opponents the fact that they were dealers in and possessors of the stuff that song and story allege makes the mare go. They wore the $ mark as a club breastplate, while the Lawyers, poor devils, reminded one of Falstaff's recruits, so variedly di-lapidated were the back number clothes they wore.

The Bankers demonstrated at an early stage of the game that they had a mortgage on the result and were determined in their characteristic, cold-blooded way to foreclose, but the Lawyers displayed their customary professional cunning by resorting to technicalities and succeeded in delaying the case for three mortal hours, Judge Foster being powerless to put a stop to this almost criminal waste of time.

The Bankers were strongest in their battery. McManus was always Johnny-on-the-Spot, just in the rear of the bat, and gathered in Westland's centrifigal curves with the utmost ease. He had plenty of work to do, for rarely did the Lawyers find them; in fact, they couldn't have hit Westland if he had been throwing street cars over the plate.

On the other hand, the Bankers knocked Clark out of the box at every opportunity, and his bruised and bleeding personality was scattered all over the diamond.

It was somewhere along about the fourth inning that Mr. Alonzo Taylor picked up the willow for the Bankers. He was accorded an enthusiastic greeting by his hosts of admirers on the cushioned seats, led off by the cow bell orchestra and received many floral tributes, the most noticeable being a lovely skunk cabbage. Inspired by this reception, he braced himself for a supreme effort and blasted Clark's first delivery over towards Church & LaMoure's Addition at an angle of forty-five degrees and at a rate of 4,000 miles to the minute. The ball flew up towards the blue empyrean beyond the range of human vision and the general verdict was that it had gone to join the angels, but finally the immutable law of gravity reversed its upward trajectory and dropped it like a dislodged meteor to Mother Earth. Judge Clark saw it coming and made a bluff to intercept it but happened to remember that in the law of falling bodies the velocity increases in inverse ratio to the distance, and fearing the result should it come in contact with his lily white hands, stepped to one side and let it bury itself in a granite boulder.

Taylor reached second and stopped to give the ladies a chance to admire the Hercules who had come so near knocking out a law of nature. Everybody on the Bankers followed suit, finding the ball and sending it flying to the four winds of heaven. The fielders thought it was raining baseballs and called for umbrellas.

And so it went, from 3:30 to half past six. But why dwell upon the horrible details? Only an abnormal appetite craves such rank mental food. The result was as stated above. Let that suffice.

Bay Siders the Champions

River Siders Defeated by the Score of 28 to 27

Red Hot Base Ball Game

The feature of the ball game was A.J. Westland's batting for the River Siders. He would step up to the plate and the first ball that would come his way he would smash square in the nose. Away the spherical hog hide would go, sailing over the heads of the astonished outfielders and over the fence. Finally, a mounted patrol was organized on the outside of the grounds to chase his sky fliers. When he first went to bat two men were on base. He swung the willow and the ball landed in a tray of dough over in the Scandinavian Methodist Episcopal church parsonage kitchen. The next time he faced the pitcher the bases were full and he sent the ball on an aerial voyage through the thin upper stratas. The law of gravitation got in its work over on Twenty-second and Colby, and as it neared the earth the ball struck one of Linton's horses that had escaped from the stable, killing it instantly. The River Siders scored four.

In discouraging contrast to this magnificent work was the inexcusably rotten performance of H.D. Cooley of the Bay Siders. He fanned the ambient air three times without ever getting in the same ward with the ball. He couldn't have hit a brick block had it been sent over the plate by a Kansas cyclone. Finally he was given a base on balls, reached second by an accident, tried to steal third, was caught in the act and sent to the bench. Cooley couldn't steal a door mat from a vacant house in Snohomish. His law partner, Judge Horan, who occupied a prominent seat in the grand stand, hung his head with mortification. Cooley is strictly in it when it comes to practicing law, but he can't play ball even a little bit.

Westland pitched for the River Siders and the ladies declared that his living picture posings were out of sight. Batsmen who faced him were not at all stuck on his style; they couldn't find him, couldn't get on to his curves. They liked Kirmse much better—he relieved Westland in the fourth inning—and showed their appreciation by pounding him into a shapeless, quivering mass, knocking the stuffing and nine runs out of his work. Fuller, weight 290 pounds avoirdupois, covered second for the River Siders, completely.

Joe Swalwell of the River Siders was voted, on a straw ballot by the ladies present, to be the best looking man on the diamond. He came very near catching a fly once, but just as the ball was about to come in contact with his lily white hands, he was struck by a double flash of lightning from a pair of eyes in the grand stand and stood there hypnotized.

The game was played with two umpires, Gardiner for the Bay Side boys and McManus for the River Side. Both showed considerable zeal in giving their nines the benefit of any doubts. The final score was 28 to 27 in favor of the Bay Side.

The ball landed in a tray of dough in the parsonage kitchen

Puget Mill Company "Clowns" beat "Veribest" 10 to 8.

Is Marriage a Failure?

Interesting Test To Be Made In A Ball Game Between A Team Of Benedicts And A Gang Of Bucks

It is now ordained that the Bachelors and Married Men will come together in mortal combat next Wednesday afternoon—at the fair grounds in a nine inning ball game — that is if they last that long. Preparations are being made for the struggle which is expected to release many women from irksome matrimonial bonds and save unmarried ladies from future unhappiness. Two hearses and an ambulance will be on tap together with Doc Wainwright's well known surgical ability. Never before in the history of baseball in this city have arrangements been made for a match so carefully as for this game between the bachelors and married men. It is stated that since the ladies, both married and unmarried, have learned how much danger is expected from this match they have been endeavoring to coax their husbands and prospective lords to get in the game.

One lady whose husband has been addicted to slot machines, highballs and other unholy diversions, said in an interview today: "Of course I don't want you to use my name in the public print, but this is a rare opportunity for ladies of homicidal proclivities to free themselves of side kickers who are not all they should be; also for young unmarried women to disconnect themselves from languishing swains who make goo-goo eyes and want to drink soda water with them from the same straw. I've been there and I know what it is; it's bad enough, but not so bad as married life, and this chance of freedom is too bright not to be hugged to the bosom of nearly every married woman in Everett. If my husband can't play I want him to umpire, because I believe there will be the same casualties there."

In the firing line the single and double warriors are to be arrayed in a Joseph-like assortment of uniforms, which will beyond doubt show them up to the best possible advantage.

It is expected that at least $200 will be realized for the library and from this amount surgical operations and funeral expenses are not to be deducted. The wives have gladly offered to stand good for all such accounts.

Ghastly Struggle is On

Ball Park Is Now the Arena of What is Destined To Be the Bull Run and Appomattox for Somebody

Tomorrow the Herald will publish a full and complete list of killed and wounded resulting from the ball game this afternoon between the married men and single men. An ambulance and trained hospital corps attended on the firing line. It is not known what kind of medicine was administered. Insinuations have been made, but there is always a temperance crank or two in any gathering.

The warriors arrived on the battlefield at 1:30 o'clock for practice. They needed it. Captain Taylor's single men lined up in abbreviated pants and dance hall lingerie, while Captain Swalwell's team were arrayed in docked trousers and wonderful hosiery giving them the appearance of harlequins. Oh yes, Captain Taylor sported silk garters which called forth envious remarks from the grandstand. Captain Taylor, by the way, is accused of betting eagles and half eagles on both teams.

The grandstand and bleachers were thronged by the wealthy and cultured and other people. The colors of the contending teams were fairly equally distributed. The man who owed his tailor a bill was not afraid of the man of cloth and tapeline; the physician conversed or yelled with the horse doctor—class and class distinction was lost in the excitement and desire of the bloody carnage. During a rest Captain Swalwell received a telegram and the crowd feared Governor McBride was putting a stop to the battle, but it was only word from a man to whom Captain Swalwell owed money and who didn't want him to play.

In the language of Mr. Dooley:

"'Tis a ghreat ghame, Hennessy, an' I wud rhather hev seen it thin th' coronation av' me old friend King Eddie!"

That Ball Game as Mr. Dooley Saw It

I saw a game of ball yesterday played in rag time. They called themselves Married Men and Single Men, but you couldn't tell the difference as you sat in the grand stand for they didn't have their wives in the game. Captain Taylor of the singles was one of the first on the field. He narrowly escaped being arrested when he pranced upon the turf with these pink and dizzy socks with a bewildering pattern, but he presented the cop with a fiver and was permitted to stay in the game.

Mister Walter Thornton was appointed Umpire because he couldn't play good enough for a place with the men. He was dressed in a becoming bath robe and a helmet, wearing a murderous looking pop gun in his belt with which he intimidated the players.

First at bat was Alderman Pendleton of the henpecked aggregation who took a base on balls. Strong accidentally made a safe hit but was retired while trying dishonestly to reach the second station. Pendleton ran home as fast as if he were passing an ordinance.

Fearing with good reason that murder was on, the city hospital sent down the ambulance with a load of beer. As soon as the players saw it, they all wanted to go in for repairs and were only restrained by the captains with difficulty.

When the Single Men went to bat, Kangaroo Sievers called for four high balls from Pitcher Fratt (as though Fratt was a bartender), and took his base. Sievers then purloined second but there was a dispute with the call. Umpire Thornton was forced to use his gun to get the coaches off the playing field. As Captain Taylor went gracefully up to bat he was presented with a fine floral offering consisting of cabbage and carrots from Charlie Manning's Conservatory. He rapped the ball and Sievers came in like a frightened shingle weaver. Both teams had one run when the first inning was over.

The Married Men commenced, with the aid of Umpire Thornton, to pile in the runs, and Captain Taylor, who had several million or more bet on the game, began to look like he wished he were in Minneapolis. At one time when Umpire Thornton rendered a decision in favor of the Single Men, Prosecuting Attorney Cooley ran across from the players' bench, dragging off his coat as though he were thinking of taking the case out of the hands of the jury, and I worried that he was going to commit a crime of violence until he was chased off the field by the pop gun.

It was a great game. A great game for both sides, even if one of them didn't win the gate receipts. It was a great game for the doctors and druggists, a great game for Turkish Bath men, and a great game for the cause it was played for as $185.75 was taken in for new books for the library. The Married Men won the game by a score of 22 to 14, but the Single Men could afford to be generous for they are not married yet!

Umpire Thornton used his pop gun to get the coaches off the field

BASE BALL!

Lawyers vs. Doctors

Benefit Snohomish County
Fair Association . . .

Tuesday, July 19, 3 p.m.

FAIR GROUNDS   EVERETT

July 20, 1904
Final score: Lawyers 12, Doctors 11.
Umpire: Walter Thornton

"Walter Thornton has become case hardened in the past, but after the game yesterday he quickly jumped over the back fence and disappeared up a back street. Today he spent in the mountains, waiting for the storm to subside."

The Leans and the Fats

On Decoration Day the Fats and the Leans of this city will give an exhibition of the most grotesque and interesting nature ever witnessed in the city of Snohomish, when they will contest on the diamond for the honors of the day.

There has been considerable discussion in regard to the matter of filling up the rat holes in the field, as it is feared that some of the Leans might disappear at a critical moment. The Fats insist that the field be left as it is, but want the diamond changed so that it will be down hill all the way around. Harvey James, as pitcher of the Leans, is getting in good shape, but is seriously considering whether he had better wear toe weights to hold him down. Here there is another pinch as the Fats want to use an eight-pound ball. The Fats say that their catcher can not find a mitt large enough and wants to wear a mattress; and as no mask can be found he will have to wear a bird cage.

There will be a 15 minute time limit allowed the Fats for a three-base-hit, and any ball knocked over the fence will be counted a homerun, so the player will be saved the exertion of making the circuit of the bases. The game will be the most interesting one of the season and the proceeds will go to the city library.

(The Fats prevailed, 35 to 25, and the sale of peanuts and admission tickets netted the Library Association over $100.)

SNOHOMISH, Washington, Annual Challenge Match LEANS vs. FATS Contested on Decoration Day, Early 1900s. Tam Elwell, batter.

Junior Law Students vs Senior Law Students

Supreme Court of the Diamond

This is an action to quiet title brought by the plaintiffs against the defendants for the purpose of determining who was the rightful holder of the title of Champions of Baseball.

The plaintiffs contend that the defendants' title was clouded in that defendants were unable to successfully defend their claim in an action against the Class of '04 in the year preceding this claim. And, secondly, that owing to the plaintiffs' superior skill and numbers they are the rightful owners.

Although the plaintiffs' complaint did not state sufficient facts to constitute a good cause of action, the defendants did not demur but allowed the case to go to trial on the baseball diamond.

In the course of this trial, several new questions of baseball law arose, including one of special uniqueness. The facts of this question arise as follows:

Entering the last half of the ninth inning the preponderance of evidence was in favor of the plaintiffs by a score of 9 to 6. One man was out when the pride of the Seniors, Judge Olaf Thomas Webb, came to the bat. At this stage of the trial the anxiety of the defendants was intense, as by special agreement the victors were to acquire as fees for their professional services the possession of the ball used at the trial, which in the estimation of the Court was reasonably worth ten cents.

With these facts in mind, it was especially essential that the said Olaf Thomas Webb not be ruled out by the Court (the Umpire), but be allowed to make some telling argument. This he did. As the second one of Pitcher Korstad's saliva spheres passed over the plate he wielded the willow and committed a violent battery upon the ball, making a long high flyer. While the eyes of the Court were endeavoring to follow the line of his argument, Webb, the Sage of Mukilteo, sought to shorten his course and ran on a direct line from home plate to second base. All would have been well if it had not been for the fact that in making this short cut the said Judge Olaf Thomas Webb committed a tort by negligently colliding with the Court who was occupying his rightful position behind the pitcher's box directly in the line of the course that the said Olaf Thomas Webb was traveling in his flight from home plate to second base. Not, however, being daunted by the contempt shown to the Court, he proceded to complete his circuit of the bases, but just as he arrived at third base he saw that the fielders would get the ball home before he could get there, so he stopped at third. There he was advised by A. Emerson Cross, counsel for the defendants who was coaching at third, that he must first touch first base before he could advance, and to expiate his contempt shown to the Court, Webb should make a direct cut from third base across the diamond to first base. While the ball was on its course to the catcher who was waiting to put him out at home, Webb made his dash and landed safe and serenely on first base.

The plaintiffs' lead attorney, Pitcher Korstad, and his colleagues lost their heads at such a sudden turn of events and ascended skywards. Before they had alighted the defendants had rolled in four counts.

The Court, being justified by all precedent, allowed the five-base hit of the said Judge Olaf Thomas Webb. Thus at the final tally the preponderance of evidence was cast in favor of the defendants by a score of 10 to 9, and verdict in favor of defendants, the Senior Laws, was entered.

NOTE: Ten years later Olaf Thomas Webb was Prosecuting Attorney for Snohomish County, Washington.

O. T. Webb committed a tort by negligently colliding with the umpire

Chapter Eight: Other Baseball Stories

Gambling

Gambling was a big part of sporting events in pioneer days. There were only two prominent spectator sports: Baseball and Racing. Racing included horse races, bicycle races and foot races. All these sports were excuses for gambling.

In baseball, each team might put up so much a side (often $100 each), winner take all. Then there would be side bets made by individuals. Players bet on their own games. Players on winning teams could make considerably more money on side bets than they received as their small percentage of the gate receipts. Native Americans were inveterate gamblers "and more often than not, won the money from the white man and went home to the reservation in great spirits." Even the umpires bet on games they worked.

Inevitably this led to abuses. Gamblers attempted (sometimes successfully; Stanford University in 1894) to bribe players to deliberately throw games. Fans lost confidence that games were being contested on an even playing field. It took many years of enforcing bans on players betting on games to restore a level of trust that gambling was not controlling the outcome of baseball games.

Stood in with the Gamblers

Serious Charges Against the Stanford Baseball Team

An incident of interest to baseball players and of peculiar interest to those who look upon amateur sport as a civilizing influence and upon professionalism with doubt, occurred at the second game between Stanford and Tacoma.

In this second game of the Stanford-Tacoma series, Manager Cox, Pitcher Campbell, Catcher Davey and Fielder Rea entered into a conspiracy with the tinhorn gamblers of Tacoma to throw the game. For their treachery to their colors they were to receive $500. Campbell and Davey being the battery, it looked like a sure thing, and the gambling fraternity bet heavily and secured odds, so that they would quit winners of $2,000 if Stanford lost.

Capt. Sheehan was approached with $100, but he was too thorough a gentleman and too loyal to his university to accept. The game commenced and Campbell began to toss balls over the plate. A reference to the score of that game shows that he only struck out one man of a team of weak hitters. About the middle of the game Capt. Sheehan, Lewis, McLain, Weldon and Calhoun discovered what the traitors were doing. Then commenced a fight between the honorable members of the team and the traitors—the one to win the game, the other to win the price of their treachery. Campbell even went so far as to tell the batters not to hit the ball, that he would give them the base on balls. But so easy did he send the ball across the plate that the temptation was too great, and they would knock slow ones out to Lewis, only to be thrown out at first. Sheehan, Calhoun, Lewis, Weldon and McLain played like demons. They batted like piledrivers, ran bases with desperation, caught impossible flies—and won the game.

The gamblers were a sorry lot after the game. Many had staked their last cent on the result, as a sure thing. They looked in awe at the men who had beat them out of their money and refused bribes. After the game there was a big fight in the Stanford team. The honest men declared their intention of abandoning the trip. But on promise of good behavior on the part of the conspirators, they consented not to leave. Walton and Dyer were sent for so that Rea and Davey could be dispensed with.

Cox is regarded with little favor at the university. The faculty did not wish the team to make the trip under him. His ideas on amateur athletics are not all good. Campbell has not been allowed to play any games with the university this year, he having played with the San Francisco and Oakland professional teams and therefore ruled out of university athletics. Neither he nor Cox are bona fide students at Stanford. Both have obtained leaves of absence from the university, it is generally supposed to avoid being asked to leave. The faculty refused to let Cox be a candidate for manager of the football team. Rea and Davey are men without honor. The other members of the team are fine fellows, from the best California families.

Out of regard for the men on the Stanford team who were not responsible for the disgrace, nothing has been said about the matter while the Stanford team was in the state, as it would have ruined their trip.

Scrappy Baseball

Arlington Man Tries to Win by Breaking a Snohomish Back Bone.

And a Poor Loser Knocks Down a Few and Pays a Fine for the Fun of It.

Yesterday afternoon the Arlington baseball club got a neat and nice drubbing at the hands of Snohomish, the home team. The score stood 11 to 2 when the game ended in the middle of the ninth inning. Be it said to the credit of the visiting ball players that they took their defeat like gentlemen and did very little kicking. The only exception to this was when one of the Arlington players jumped into Clemans on second and tried to break his back while Clem was catching a ball to put him out.

The rooters from Arlington, however, acted badly from the very beginning of the game, proving that the old time bad blood over games historical still flows hot in their veins. One man who bet $40 and lost, got very much riled and for a while it looked as if he would start a riot. He wasn't a game loser, or was a game loser, which ever way you look at it. After the crowd left the grounds he knocked down a man who had asked him to be quiet in the grandstand, and struck him while he was down. Then when a Snohomish man said it was a shame to strike a man when he was down, this same village blacksmith tackled him and got two good punches in the face before they went down in a clinch and were pulled apart by bystanders.

It was awfully warm for a while, but the ringleaders were arrested and fined $25. They were then allowed to go to the train, and things became calm and peaceful in the old town once more.

Shut Out Monroe

The Snohomish baseball team shut out Monroe on the Snohomish diamond Sunday by a score of 8 to 0.

The game was brought about by a boast of the Monroe fans that they could win this game, and they put up $100 to prove it. Snohomish took their money and the game. It is claimed that $400 in side money was also won.

A big crowd of fans came down from Monroe to see the game, some in rigs and some on the train. It is claimed many of the latter walked home.

It was a good, hard fought game. Stevens, the Snohomish pitcher struck out eleven men. The star play of the game was when McFarren, the new talent from Palouse, made a three bagger when the bases were full, two men were out and there were two strikes against him. He brought three men in and clinched the victory for Snohomish. A shower of silver from grand stand and bleachers showed the appreciation of the home enthusiasts. About $10 was scattered over the field.

Monroe lost the game but played good ball just the same. The batteries were: Snohomish, Stevens and Waters; Monroe, Stephens and McManus. The umpire was Smith of Snohomish.

Everett Suckers Bite and Get Bit

They Then Howl and Roar

*Bet Their Money on Sedro-Woolley
and That Bunch Deliberately Throws the Game to Everett*

About two hundred people went from Everett to Bellingham on the excursion run by the baseball team yesterday, and, it being an ideal day, the trip was greatly enjoyed although the return was somewhat later than had been expected.

But the pleasure of the trip was the only enjoyment, for the game of baseball between the Everett and Sedro-Woolley teams was certainly one of the rankest deals ever perpetrated upon the public of this or any other section of the country. It was a deliberate attempt to rob Everett people and was fixed up by the Sedro-Woolley players and the people of Bellingham.

When the crowd from Everett reached Bellingham at nearly 2 o'clock in the afternoon they were somewhat surprised to find people on every street corner who were willing to bet money that Everett would win the game. Knowing that Sedro-Woolley had not lost a single game during the season, they readily fell into the trap and could not get their money up fast enough. It was promptly covered and more asked for. Everett men were betting in good faith while Bellingham people were in with the Sedro-Woolley bunch on the deal to throw the game to Everett and thus secure the money bet.

During the first three innings of the game it looked as though a good exhibition would be witnessed, for until the last half of the third inning neither side had made a score. But then Sedro got busy and sent nine men around to score without a struggle. Then Everett got two runs, the Sedro players having absolutely quit playing, kicking the ball along when apparently trying to get hold of it and allowing Everett men to run undisturbed around the diamond.

And even then the Everett suckers continued to bite and bet. They scrambled over each other to get what looked to them like easy money.

But oh, what an awakening later when the Woolley players continued to throw the game and it was apparent that some kind of a deal was on. They howled and clamored for their money back; that all bets be declared off, which Tom Fields, as umpire, finally did, although where he got the authority is a puzzle to everybody but the suckers who got their money back, and they maintain that it was the only proper thing to do.

While all this monkey business was going on the public, which had paid its good money at the gate, groaned in agony over the worst exhibition of baseball ever witnessed. They left the grounds by the streetcar load, vowing never again to attend an exhibition of the national game.

There are those who maintain that Everett Manager Dresen was to blame for not calling the game when he saw how the Sedro men were throwing it, but, on the other hand, the question arises as to where he would have been in case he did that. Those attending the game and not betting would have howled "fake" and demanded their money back, and with perfect right, too. But, for the sake of sport, there is a question if that would not have been the best method to pursue. As the matter stands Manager Dresen feels humiliated and deplores the occurrence deeply.

One thing is certain, it will be hard to interest people in baseball to the extent they have been, for fear of a similar occurrence. There is a question as to whether the result of the game stands 9 to 9 or 11 to 10 in favor of Everett, but it makes practically no difference for the game cannot be officially recognized as one of the series to be played by the league teams.

Ballplayer Steals Wife from Pesthouse

Boards Train for Portland Scattering Smallpox Germs All Along the Route.

Through a bedroom window of the Walla Walla, Washington pesthouse, southwest of town, Ball Player Edward Hogan gallantly rescued his smallpox stricken wife, drove her to the depot and took the O.R. & N. night train for Portland.

When the pesthouse matron went to Mrs. Hogan's room she found it vacant. The window was open, however, and small footprints, guided by larger ones, both leading to tell-tale buggy tracks nearby, told the story.

Mr. Hogan got away without suspicion. At the depot he turned over the rig to Mickey Clancy, whom he asked to drive up town.

The agile center fielder was speeding toward Portland when Mickey discovered he was "stuck" for the charges.

Hogan wanted to get out because the Inland Empire League, in which he was a shining star, had broken up. He got word to Mrs. Hogan through a friend, and she wanted to go with him. She had already been twenty-four days in the pesthouse. Hogan made plans to kidnap her bodily. Scattering germs as she went, the race to the depot was a swift one. It was not generally known that Hogan's wife was isolated, and no suspicion was aroused.

Ministers Oppose Sunday Baseball

Ask Snohomish Players Not to Play Games in That Town on Sunday.

The question of baseball or no baseball on Sunday is up. The Ministerial Association has asked the players not to have a game next Sunday. The players evidently intend to play, although they do not say so in plain words in their reply, which, together with the request, is printed below.

Snohomish, May 10, 1905.

To the Snohomish Baseball Team, Gentlemen:

We, the undersigned ministers, members of the Snohomish Ministers' Association, do most respectfully petition you to defer your ball game for next Sunday, May 14, and do most cordially invite you to attend the union services to be held in the rink on that day, especially the men's meeting at 3 p.m.

Respectfully yours,
E.H. HUDSON, Pres.

Snohomish, Wash., May 10, 1905.

To the Snohomish Ministers' Association, Messrs:

Owing to previous engagements, we are compelled to most respectfully decline your very kind invitation.

C.B. SEARS, Sec.

Here follow all the signatures of the team.

Wife Wields Whip Over Ball Player

One Out-of-town Baseball Man Has a Strenuous Time

Spouse Pursues Him Relentlessly, Traces Him From Place to Place and Then Lashes Him

"You must come home, Bill Bailey," was the burden of the song which the wife of an out-of-town baseball player threw at her spouse on the streets of Everett last night. She emphasized the strong points of her command by the use of a horse whip.

The origin of the trouble is shrouded in mystery, which so often envelopes affairs of a domestic nature, that is, until they reach the limelight of the divorce court, if perchance they get that far. But the ball player last night wasn't particularly interested in motives or origins; the present, represented by the aforementioned horse whip and wife, kept him busy.

A local baseball man wanted to talk business with the out-of-town man. The two began walking from the hotel where they were stopping, up Hewitt Avenue. That was late at night. Before they had gone far, the pursuing wife was after them. The local man, being wise, walked ahead, and left his guest to face the music. That squall blew over and the visitor again rejoined the Everett man.

But it was only the prelude. Hardly had they found a resting place in the rear of a saloon, where they could talk business, when the wife again appeared. There was another scene. The wife demanded that the husband at once move hotelward. It was promised that that should be done in a short time, and she once more departed. The baseball men thought best to change headquarters. They sought another rear room, but again did the relentless wife pursue them, this time in a hack. Breathlessly they awaited for her arrival, but no sound was heard. Finally, after ten minutes had passed, they made bold to speak above a whisper. Then the storm burst upon them. This time the wife entered armed with a whip. All three departed hurriedly, and there on a sidestreet, just off Hewitt, was the whip called into action.

Once more was peace patched up, although the husband by this time declared he wouldn't go home. Apparently he was annoyed by his wife's tactics. An armistice being agreed upon, the wife retired temporarily from the scene of action.

The baseball man, though, didn't feel like humoring his wife's whim just yet; besides, the business talk wasn't completed.

The local man advised him to make for the hotel without further delay, but he wasn't ready to do so.

They moved on to another stopping place, only to once more hear the rattle of the hack, the driver of which seemed to be able to intuitively keep upon their trail. There was another clash. The local man thought things were too strenuous and bade goodnight and departed. It is supposed that "Bill Bailey" went home.

Bellingham manager's wife wields the whip

Manager Drennan Fined for Beating His Wife

Kirby J. Drennan, captain and manager of the Bellingham team of the Northwest Baseball League, appeared in the police court in a new role yesterday morning. His wife also appeared, with a black eye, and charged that it was due to blows from her husband's fist.

The result was a fine of $75 and costs assessed against the baseball man by Judge Williams.

Mrs. Drennan said her husband was a considerate man when sober, but that Sunday night he had been drinking heavily. On coming home he attacked her in a ferocious manner, blackening her eyes and striking her several blows. She said her body was black and blue, and declared he had whipped her again yesterday morning, after which she determined to swear out the warrant.

Drennan admitted he was probably guilty. He declared that his wife had entered a saloon where he was drinking with a party of other men, last night, and that angered him.

Funeral Clouds Drape Bellingham

Once more Bellingham seems to be in the slough of despond

Dark clouds of funereal hue have gathered about Whatcom County fandom, and the faithful are preparing to sit in sackcloth and ashes. They cry with a loud voice: "We have been deceived; woe unto us;" then they raise their voices again in agony of lamentation and say, "Behold Manager Kirby Drennan's social standing."

This is not an exaggeration. Would that it were. It is all vouched for by a Bellingham evening newspaper.

The result has been that the money offered by Bellingham men for their team is not yet forthcoming.

Sad to relate, Kirby Drennan's social standing is objected to. Kirby recently visited the police court in Bellingham. While there he paid a $75 fine for beating his wife while intoxicated.

Parenthetically, it might be remarked that in Everett over a month ago the situation was reversed. It was Kirby's wife that undertook the horsewhip role, and she wielded the rawhide strenuously.

But, so it is stated, some of the subscribers object to paying out their cash to help support a team that is managed by a patron of the police court. They are even offended at Director Miller, "says the Bellingham paper,"because of the report that he paid Drennan's fine and expressed sympathy for him."

"All things considered," the paper says, "the club seems to be right up against it."

Two Ball Players Fight with an Officer

Pitcher Charlie Shields Knocks a Negro Senseless for Eating at Street Lunch Counter Beside Him

He Resists Arrest, With Aid of Cliff Blankenship, Who Holds Policeman While Former Punches Him

Patrolman King, After Stiff Fight, Lays Out One Player and Takes Both to Jail—Are Released on Bail.

Charlie Shields and Cliff Blankenship, of the Seattle baseball team, permitted their rowdy tendencies to get the best of them Sunday morning. Both are now under arrest, Shields being booked at police headquarters for disorderly conduct and Blankenship for interfering with an officer. They are to be tried in the police court this afternoon. Meanwhile, they are at liberty on $20 bail each.

The two ball players gave their exhibition, and incidentally indicated why the Seattle team keeps at the tail end of the standings, about 3 o'clock Sunday morning. Because a negro sailor had the audacity to stand beside the ball players at a public lunch stand on the corner of Washington Street and Second Avenue South at which they were eating, Shields beat him into insensibility. Patrolman Jack King saw him fall and rushed across the street to arrest his assailant. The minute King appeared Shields started to beat him. When the officer attempted to defend himself Blankenship threw his arms around King's neck and held him while his companion struck him. Although the odds were against King, he succeeded after a hard struggle in knocking Shields down and out with his fists. He then placed the handcuffs on Shields and sent both men to headquarters.

When Shields reached headquarters he presented a pitiable appearance as the result of his encounter with the police officer. His left cheek was swollen to twice its natural size, and the side of his nose was smashed as if it had been struck with a hammer. He had several other bruises on his face. King's memento of the battle with the two ball players consisted of but a scratch on the neck given him by Blankenship and a soiled helmet. When being booked, Shields persisted in telling King that he would "get even" with him. The patrolman simply laughed and said: "You can fight policemen just about as well as you play ball."

Shields was considerably under the influence of liquor at the time, but Blankenship appeared in condition to know what he was doing.

Blankenship has previously given exhibitions of rowdiness in Seattle, but this is Shields' first public appearance as a tough. Last season Blankenship assaulted a well-known sporting writer who had criticised his careless playing and was laid off for several days for his conduct. Later, while playing with the Cincinnati team, he was in trouble for fighting.

General Manager Agnew, of the Seattle team, announced this afternoon that Shields had been fined $100 by the management and indefinitely suspended as the result of the scrap. On investigation Mr. Agnew found that Shields was wholly to blame, and he was punished accordingly. Blankenship, Agnew says, only interfered to protect Shields.

Shields and Blankenship

Shields and Blankenship were two of the best players on a moribund Seattle Siwashes team which finished last in the Pacific Coast League in 1905.

They both played in the Major Leagues (albeit briefly) both before and after the fighting episode.

On July 8, 1905, Charlie Shields had set a Pacific Coast League record by striking out 19 Portland batters in a 5 to 1 Seattle victory. This game also featured the Portland pitcher who, after giving up a home run, "walked to the bench, put on his coat, and walked out of the grounds."

The Seattle Daily Times reported that "since his recent escapade Shields has been working like a major, running around the park every morning so many times that he makes his friends dizzy, with the result that he is in better shape now than at any time since last spring. Charlie is anxious to redeem himself in the estimation of his friend and manager, Russ Hall, and he may be given a chance later."

After a month, the repentant Shields was considered sufficiently rehabilitated to be given the ball to pitch the final home game of the Seattle season. He came through with a masterful 3 to 0 shutout of Oakland.

Earlier in the year the *Times* had said of Blankenship: "This lad comes mighty near being half of the Seattle team, with his fine catching, his ginger on the bases and his timely hitting."

STANWOOD TIDINGS • SNOHOMISH COUNTY, WASHINGTON • SUMMER 1905

Stanwood Newspaper Editor

Back in nineteen-o-five, Stanwood had a very good amateur baseball team. The team received lengthy front page coverage from the editor of the *Stanwood Tidings* newspaper; Stanwood's opponents, however, were often targets for the editor's fiery pen.

In May, 1905, Stanwood lost a game at Arlington on a missed call by the umpire. The self-righteous editor wrote:

"Stanwood does not care to win a ball game by questionable umpiring. Our sister town, however, is not a whit more particular now than in the past, when the very name Arlington was a stench in the nostrils of honest and decent people.'

In June of 1905, the editor reported on a trip for a game at Milltown:

"The ball team went in a wagon as far as the Skagit County line. At that point the wagon road comes to an abrupt end, so the boys walked on into Milltown. The condition of the roads in that portion of Skagit County is a lasting disgrace, and whoever is responsible deserves to be fired out of office and kept out!"

Then in August, 1905, Stanwood traveled to Snohomish for a game. After the Snohomish players had roughed up the umpire and pelted the departing Stanwood players with eggs, the outraged Stanwood editor wrote:

"The Snohomish baseball outfit is a disgrace to the town, to Snohomish County, and to the State of Washington. That outfit has no regard for truth, decency, or baseball ethics... The City of Snohomish was disgraced by these men last Sunday. The stain of that day cannot be wiped out in years!"

Howlett Loses Bunch of Cash

Handed Mrs. Howlett $221 in Paper Money; Cash is Missed Soon Afterwards

The loss of $221 by George Howlett, member of the Bellingham baseball team and former manager of the Victoria nine, was reported Sunday evening to the police. The latter have investigated, but have been able to learn nothing.

According to the story told the police, Mr. Howlett gave his wife the money a few minutes before 12 o'clock while they were in their room in the Manila Hotel. The sum was in paper in a small pocketbook. A few minutes before 2 o'clock Mrs. Howlett missed it. A thorough search was at once made, but the missing money was nowhere to be found.

Mrs. Howlett does not remember distinctly where she placed the pocketbook. She was out of the room but twice, to go to the kitchen, before the money was missed. No one else, it was reported, had been in the room except the chamber maid, and she was in only when either Mr. or Mrs. Howlett was there.

Howlett had to leave soon after the loss was discovered, to go to the ball grounds, where he pitched yesterday's game,* but the search continued all afternoon. The police were not notified until 6 o'clock, as it was thought the purse would be found somewhere about the room.

The Seattle Daily Daily Times, reporting the same incident, said:

"Ball players should not leave their money with their wives. Some ball players never have any money. Others haven't any wives. George Howlett had both money and a wife. Now he has only his wife and a hard luck story. The two shouldn't go together, but they do in Howlett's case."

* Howlett was the losing pitcher in Bellingham's loss to Everett, 6 to 2.

Stanwood's Catcher Drowned

Stanwood was to have played the Twin Cities on the Arlington grounds tomorrow, but owing to the drowning of Stanwood's catcher, Johnnie Abbott, the game is off. Abbott, who is a halfbreed from Skagit City, got into a fight at Mount Vernon on Thursday and was arrested by the city marshal. While the marshal was taking him to the lockup, Abbott broke away and ran and jumped into the Skagit River, the marshal pursuing him in a boat. After swimming for half a mile Abbott went under a boomstick and was drowned. Abbott had a habit of cleaning out saloons, and three years ago was shot twice while resisting arrest.

Chapter Nine: Player Biographical Sketches

Noble Harvey (1873 - 1952)

Noble Harvey was born in June, 1873, allegedly the first white boy born in Snohomish County, Washington Territory. He was born on the 160 acre family farm which his father had purchased from the original homesteader for a total of $50.

The picture shows Noble Harvey at age 10 wearing the uniform of his first baseball team, the "Fearnaughts." The portrait was taken in the "Palace Floating Gallery," a barge-like photo studio which plied the waters of Puget Sound and its tributaries, photographing and selling "Instantaneous Portraits & Landscapes."

Noble played on some Snohomish baseball teams — usually at first base. He was a regular in the annual "Fats vs. Leans" challenge matches, having grown into his position on the "Fats" aggregation.

In 1904 Snohomish was without a baseball field, so Noble Harvey, having inherited the family farm, agreed to "build and equip a first-class ball ground" on his land. The improvements were financed by selling 60 season tickets at $5 each, the $300 being paid to Mr. Harvey upon completion of the fences, grand stand and grounds.

The Harvey farm is now the site of the Harvey Airfield in Snohomish.

Walter M. Thornton (1875-1960)

Walter Thornton was the first baseball player from Snohomish County, Washington, to play in the Major Leagues.

Walter, like most everyone in Territorial days, came from someplace else. He was born in Peoria, Illinois, in February, 1875, was orphaned at an early age, and came West to live with an older brother in Snohomish. He quickly established himself as a natural athlete skilled in several sports, but particularly in baseball. In 1893 Snohomish, with Walter Thornton pitching, won the amateur championship of Washington State. The next year, 1894, Thornton pitched the Seattle Athletic Club to the amateur championship of the entire West Coast.

In the Spring of 1895, two graduates of Cornell College, Mount Vernon, Iowa, who were co-owners of the *Snohomish Tribune* newspaper, arranged a full-ride financial package for Thornton to attend Cornell. He arrived on campus in time for the baseball season, and so distinguished himself against collegiate competition that he was invited for a try-out with the Chicago Colts (later Cubs) of the National League. He was promptly signed to join the Colts after school was out in June. He spent the summer of 1895 in the Chicago organization, and made his major league pitching debut on July 1st, 1895. The Chicago sportswriters wrote glowing reports about Thornton's potential.

Thornton returned to Cornell in the fall of 1895 and plunged back into student life. He was elected President of the Freshman Class and was initiated into one of the College societies.

Thornton pitched and won at least one game for Cornell in October, 1895. Using professionals to play for college teams did not seem quite fair, so in December, 1895, the Amateur Athletic Union passed a rule banning the use of a professional battery by amateur baseball teams. This ended Thornton's college athletic career, much to the disappointment of the Cornell fans.

In March of 1896, Thornton left Cornell to join the Chicago baseball team for spring training in Galveston. In June of 1896, Thornton further distinguished himself by marrying one of his teachers at Cornell, Mrs. Sarah Andrews Hackett, Director of the School of Oratory and Physical Culture. He was 21, she was 26.

The high point of Thornton's baseball career occurred on August 21, 1898, when he pitched a no-hit, no-run game against Brooklyn. When he wasn't pitching, Thornton played in the outfield and compiled a career major league batting average of .312 in over 500 at-bats. Thornton's major league career was unfortunately cut short after only four seasons because of a contract dispute with the owner of the Chicago team.

After pitching for Seattle in 1899, Thornton moved to Everett where he, acting as Manager and Captain, assembled the great Everett team of 1901—the team that won its first 27 games in a row. Thornton had injured his pitching arm so he played first base and batted over .500 for the 1901 season. He retired from playing baseball after the 1902 season.

In 1910, the evangelist and former ballplayer Billy Sunday came to Everett for a six weeks religious campaign. Although he at first resisted, Walter Thornton eventually came under the spell of Billy Sunday and became a life-long follower of Billy Sunday and of Jesus Christ.

After Thornton's wife died around 1920, he moved to Los Angeles and became a street preacher to the down-and-outers on Skid Row. In this blighted "section of sorrow" Thornton became a fixture —a steady figure of power in a Skid Row of beaten men. Night after night he walked to the Midnight Mission in the heart of the "city without a heart" and preached to the hungry men who clamored for his words of encouragement.

Finally the ravages of age overpowered the old warrior. In July, 1960, a press release reported that at age 85 Walter Thornton died all alone in his hotel room, "and there he soared to the diamond in the skies."

Walter Thornton and the Bagpiper

A bagpipe player has been holding forth in various saloons along Front Street several evenings this week. The music is agreeable when the listener is far out of range of it.

Two youths were arrested Monday night for shying an apple into James Graham's saloon in the Edmond Block, where Phaedrig na Pib was playing the pipes. Their intention was to hit Phaedrig, but instead they broke a window in the rear door. In mitigation of the offense it may be said that the provocation was great and that the aim was tolerably good.

The facts showed that the apple, starting 30 feet from the door, had entered the premises at an elevation not above 7 feet. On nearly the same level it had traveled the length of the saloon, at least 40 feet, and had passed through the rear window some four feet from the floor.

The saloonkeeper knew that no one in town but Walter Thornton could make a throw like that. He therefore took counsel of the City Marshal, who straightway found Walter and summoned him for malicious mischief.

Thornton went up and settled last night. He paid one dollar to the owner of the broken pane.

(Walter Thornton was 16 years old.)

THE SEATTLE TELEGRAPH • SEATTLE, WASHINGTON • AUGUST 6, 1894

"Snohomish" Thornton

Fine Ball Tosser, an "Amoosin" Cuss and a Good Fellow

Walter M. Thornton is the name of the young man who has made such a fine record in pitching the champion Seattle Athletic Club nine on to victory this season. He is a strapping big fellow, over six feet tall and weighing over 170 pounds, yet he is only a lad in years. The young Snohomish southpaw, as he is popularly known in Seattle, was born in Peoria, Illinois in 1875. With his family he moved to Snohomish early in the year 1890, and there he has lived until he came to Seattle this summer for the purpose of studying in preparation for college. He jokingly says of himself that he has played ball ever since he was able to carry one. He played on the Snohomish nine during the seasons of '91 and '92, but it was not until '93 that he made a record for himself by not only pitching for, but captaining that nine and winning the amateur championship of the Sound. This season he has gone one better and pitched in nearly all the games of the club winning the amateur championship of the Pacific Coast.

Thornton is a pitcher of unusual ability. He has tremendous speed, a quick, deep drop and an easy delivery. Lefthanded as he is, his lightning jump ball alone is enough to deceive most batsmen, but this, combined with his toboggan shoot, makes monkeys of an average team. He is a good all-round player as well as pitcher. He runs like a deer, knows how to bat, and is acquainted with all the fine points of the game. He is an enthusiastic player, entering into the game with zest, and has none of the elements of a disorganizer in his system.

This youngster is not only a ball tosser of ability, but he has other qualities. He has native wit and humor to a high degree. Given a group of men who have nothing particular to do and let "Snohomish" loose on them, and in five minutes you will find him the center of attraction, entertaining, convulsing one and all by his repartee, story telling and awkward, funny dances.

Quick to learn and already possessed of a good general knowledge, young Thornton proposes to make his way further in educational matters, if this be possible. With his ability and host of friends, this youngster is pretty sure to go on to very decent things, both in an athletic way and otherwise.

Thornton shying an apple at the bagpaper

Gastronomic Feats of Ball Players

By Hugh S. Fullerton

Perhaps the best feeder that ever broke into the game was Walter Thornton, the big pitcher who starred with Anson a couple of years and was driven out of baseball because he declined to sign a contract at the terms offered him by Colonel Hart of Chicago.

Thornton was big and vulgarly healthy, and never was there such an appetite. He could spot Bill Everitt two lamb chops and a dish of peas and beat him easily, which in itself was going some. Not only did he hold the championship for a single meal, but he was one of the most persistent eaters that ever happened. He was a trifle handicapped because he used only a fork in eating, which gave some of the knife manipulators an advantage, but he was there. Many times at night when the train was running along with the lights out in the sleepers and everybody seemingly dead to the world, the train would stop and any one who was awake would hear a window lifted cautiously and then Thornton's voice would ask: "Say boy, is there any place near here you can get me a sandwich?"

One extremely hot day in Philadelphia Thornton pitched two games in one afternoon. The heat was intense; so great that Frank Chance, who was catching him, was wading in water and mud caused from perspiration dripping from his uniform. The players of both teams were suffering intensely. During the second game I dropped down to the bench to speak to someone and T. Donahue met me with: "What do you think of him?"

"He's going along pretty well," I responded.

"I don't mean pitching," said T. "I mean eating. He's eaten a sandwich every two innings since he started, and now he's gone in after a piece of pie!"

Descriptions of the Baseball Scene (1894-1901)
Various Sportswriters, Various Newspapers

(all were games in which Walter Thornton played)

THE SEATTLE POST-INTELLIGENCER, June 3, 1894:
"With the sun shining clear in the heavens, the home team jumped into the lead and pranced along like a 3-year-old horse with his tail over the dashboard."

THE PORTLAND OREGONIAN, July 29, 1894:
"Thornton came to Portland from Snohomish well-stocked with curves and shoots, and with more speed than a coyote en route to a sheep ranch."

THE SNOHOMISH EYE, July 11, 1895: (Quoting the *Chicago Inter Ocean*) "Anson put Thornton in to bat in the fifth inning. The crowd became as attentive as a congregation when a woman with a pretty bonnet comes in late."

"In speed and curves Thornton has an assortment large enough to stock a department store, but he is as wild as a minister's son."

THE SEATTLE DAILY TIMES, June 11, 1900:
"The sensational feature of the day came in the eighth inning when Thornton hit for what looked like a homer to right center. Wooden turned and ran like a belated passenger trying to catch a trolley, and, sticking up his mitt, the ball nestled in as though it had tired of its aerial flight."

EVERETT DAILY HERALD, June 12, 1901:
"In the last half of the eighth the Spokane Bunchgrassers looked as though they had been caught stealing sheep."

Thomas P. Bird (1873-1955)

Tom Bird was born in Saginaw, Michigan in 1873 and died at Seattle, Washington in 1955 at age 82. Between those years he had an incredibly varied career while maintaining some involvement with baseball until he was over 75 years old.

The Bird family moved to a homestead near Snohomish, Washington Territory in the late 1880's. Tom played on his first baseball team when he was in the fifth grade.

In 1893 Tom was Walter Thornton's catcher on the championship Snohomish ball club. Later in the 1890's he attended the University of Washington and caught for the University team.

In 1898 Tom enlisted in the First Montana Volunteer Cavalry and fought with Teddy Roosevelt's Rough Riders in the Spanish American War. His unit trained in Florida where Tom helped organize a winning baseball team. When asked about his experiences in the war, he quipped, "I did what we all did. I loaded, fired, and ran!"

He worked on a construction gang digging the Panama Canal, and also worked with the Anaconda Copper Co. in Montana.

In 1902 Tom decided he had had enough hard, dangerous adventuring, so he enrolled in the University of Michigan Law School. While in law school he was the catcher for Michigan's varsity baseball team.

During the summers he played baseball with various teams including Seattle. In 1905 he graduated from law school and then played with Buffalo and Montreal in the Eastern League. Tom described his baseball career as "from school to sandlot to sticks to bush to minors."

He came back to Western Washington, was admitted to the bar, and in 1908 was elected to the Washington State House of Representatives. He was reelected in 1910 but declined to run in 1912.

Bird's primary business interests were in the forest products industry, but as was true for many people in small towns, he wore several hats. He served variously as the Tolt city clerk and police judge, was President and manager of the local water, light and power company, and sold real estate and insurance. He also found time to coach the Tolt high school football, track and baseball teams.

He continued to play baseball for local teams, and was reported to have played a game at third base when he was 51 years old. "The elderly, but still graceful Bird handled six or seven difficult chances flawlessly and...leaped over the Everett bats to stab barehanded a foul fly in front of the enemy dugout."

Toward the end of his life T. Bird commented, "I've lost all my money, but I've kept all my illusions."

A Rough Rider

Tom Bird Home From Santiago

Thrilling Experience in Battle

The many friends of Tom Bird were joyfully surprised last Sunday to hear that he had returned home. Nothing had been heard of his whereabouts and his family and friends have feared that he was dead. Knowing that the *Tibune* readers would be pleased to hear from Tom himself, we asked him for his story. The following is about as he saw it:

I enlisted last April with Troop 1 of Roosevelt's Rough Riders. We drilled for six weeks at Tampa before leaving for the front. At Tampa we had a varied experience and combined drilling, baseball and "copping out" watermelons.

The Rough Riders' baseball team was really the only plank in the sidewalk, and contained many players who had gained reputations in many different corners of the earth; some at colleges; some at athletic clubs; and as some had seen service on a league team, it was not a difficult matter to test a pretty fast heat, which they certainly did. I didn't know much about war, but could usually manage to see that the umpire didn't give us anything "queer" in the baseball line. We won every game we played except one, which we had hopelessly lost when God and the rain saved our reputation and what coin we had on the game.

We left Tampa on the night of the 12th of June and arrived at Siboney ten days later. When we were ready to land, the boys were fairly wild and lost no time in leaving the cramped quarters on board the *Gussie*. The pack mules were thrown overboard and made to swim ashore, and many of the men chose the same way of reaching Spanish soil.

Our regiment was safely landed and camped all night about three miles from Siboney. The next day found us on the march, and after repeated stops we arrived at a point about six miles from Siboney, where the first battle of the campaign was fought.

The firing was commenced by the Spaniards, and for over half an hour we lay in the long grass trying to figure out their exact position. The smokeless powder made this a matter of difficulty. We were protected by the tall grass which reached nearly to our ears, and by laying flat on the ground we managed to keep our bodies out of danger to a certain extent. The Spanish occupied elevated ground about 400 yards in front, and had the advantage of being able to locate our exact positions by the depressions in the grass which could easily be seen from the hilltop.

Things were in this shape when the order to charge was given, and for a few minutes it looked like a 100 yard dash with 600 starters.

The Spaniards finally left their position and retreated about two miles down the country. The ground captured was literally carpeted with shell casings; I guess if we had remained on the low ground for an hour or two there wouldn't have been a corporal's guard left.

From June 27th hence it was march or fight all day and dig trenches at night until July 3rd, when the last engagement took place. It was an attempt by the Spaniards to retake the hill captured earlier in the day by the 71st, N.Y. With clubbed guns the boys drove the Spanish out of the trenches and down into the woods. In just about two and one-half minutes the last battle on Cuban soil was won, and over 800 Spaniards were buried next morning.

We suffered mostly from the extreme heat, which caused us to perspire almost continually. We were soon reduced to skin and bones, with hardly strength enough to pack a gun. Cocoanut milk and mangoes afforded us more nourishment than anything else and kept us from starving to death, until July 9th, when we received a few supplies.

Dysentery caught hold of most of the boys while on the Island, and its weakening influence was soon apparent as on July 3rd hardly half the regiment were able to shoot a gun.

I was taken to the Red Cross hospital on July 14th, and left on the 20th on the *Yale* for New York, arriving there on the 26th. We were given quite an ovation on landing, and my trip across the continent from Jersey City to Puget Sound was a very pleasant one.

You can be sure that I will get in no more wars, and my patriotism will in the future be directed to making political speeches in the opera house. I have had enough tramping on an empty stomach to do me for the rest of my life.

Snohomish Takes Another Game from Monroe

Another whitewash for Monroe administered by Snohomish yesterday made the good people of the reformatory city decidedly sick, and made a total of twenty-six innings played by Snohomish without the opposition scoring. It was a game played on new plowed ground which accounted for errors.

The final score was Snohomish 6, Monroe 0.

Bird's Error

Capt. Tom Bird, invincible and infallible, made an error in the ball game with Monroe yesterday, and in extenuation of the paradoxical event, offered a hot excuse. He said:

"You can charge me with an error, all right, and I presume I shouldn't kick, but it happened this way. I was hiking over the mellow soil—fresh from the plow or I'm no rustic—and when I got to the place where the ball was, there it wasn't. I said to myself: 'When a ball isn't where it is, it must have sunk.' So I dived for it in the billowy loam, and found it, but it wasn't it at all. Sure it was a bloody onion. The sight of it brought tears, and when I dug up the real article, well, it was too late, thanks to the blooming Dutch tuberose."

That error stands of record against Tom and Manager Lysons says: "Tom may be a ball player and a bird, but the next time he loses the trail of the ball and goes off on the scent of an onion I'll retire him to the rustic regions where he can burrow after spuds!"

Fred C. Schock (1877-1928)

F.C. Schock, whose remarkable pitching performances in the northwestern states made him the Matthewson of that part of the country, has not had professional experience, but his admirers think that all he needs to make a reputation as one of the star twirlers of the game is a chance in fast company. He was with Walter Thornton's independent team at Everett, Wash., last year and in 14 games was credited with 136 strike outs. He pitched his first match game in 1897 for the Upper Iowa University against Cornell College and defeated them. He was the star twirler for the Upper Iowa team until 1900, when he went to the Pacific Northwest. He was a member of the University of Washington team, and later secured an engagement with the Everett team. He is six feet tall and weighs 210 pounds when in condition. His success as a pitcher is due to his great speed and fine control.

He Broke the HooDoo

Big Babe Schoch Wins Another Game

Not Only Pitched Good Ball But Also Lined Out a Couple Good Ones

Big Babe Schoch, the Amos Rusie of the Pacific Coast League, broke the hoodoo at the ball park yesterday afternoon, and not only pitched ball that at times had the Stars up in cloudlets, but he won his game beyond the shadow of a doubt in the seventh when, with two gone and two on the bases, he smashed out a sizzler to center field—his second by the way — and sent both his team mates home.

That gave the Seattle Siwashes a lead that the 'Friscoans could not overcome. The final score was Seattle 8, San Francisco 7.

Local fans are inclined to look upon this man Schoch with gentle awe. He has taken off some flesh since the season started and now tips the scales at 225 pounds. He is remarkably quick for so large a man, and speed? A wireless telegram shooting through the ether that surrounds the whirly worlds would be water-logged and driftwood in comparison with Big Babe's benders.

All his life Schoch has depended upon this same speed. Since the season opened, however, he has discovered that a man must have something else up his sleeve— He asked Manager (and catcher) Parke Wilson to go to the park with him every morning while he practiced up on a crossfire and a slow ball. Yesterday he used that slow ball in great shape. He can't control it well as yet, and that is why he gave eight passes to the initial pillow, but during the latter part of the game he coaxed it into working nicely, and he actually made Henry's men look like dubs. Schoch will do. He is hitting like a fiend and so far has been the winningest pitcher on Seattle's team.

NOTE: Later in the season Schoch injured his arm and never fully recovered.

Fred Schoch

A San Francisco paper took the following fall out of Schoch the day he pitched there;

"If Mr. Schoch ever attempts to pitch ball here again there will be a rough house. When he loomed up on that mound as big as a house and commenced to throw 'em up to the plate the fans were on to him and they were not slow in inviting him to take to the bushy districts. But he stayed—stayed so long that the game became a tragedy instead of a comedy.

"He gave the worst exhibition of any pitcher who ever toed the mountain at Recreation Park. He shocked the fans so badly that most of them made their getaways early. He shocked his teammates to such an extent that they were unable to stop a ball if it happened to be hit. He shocked Umpire Dave Cramer till the latter forgot to call strikes when they came over the plate.

"Schoch did nothing but treat batsmen to bases on balls and when he had succeeded in filling up the bases someone generally clouted the leather out to the flagpole and then the whole bunch would trot in. This sort of thing went on for seven innings, though the fans fairly begged Parke Wilson to take his ponderous joke out of the box and put in some one who could and would put a ball over the plate. Finally young Mr. Hall was trotted out. He proved so nervous and so rattled that he passed four in a row and allowed a two-bagger."

How soon the mighty have fallen!

Fred Schoch Dies Suddenly at Golf Club in Seattle

Snohomish County Stunned by Death of Leading Citizen

Fred C. Schoch, one of Everett's most influential business men and spirited public workers for more than a quarter of a century, died suddenly Wednesday afternoon while golfing at the Sand Point links at Seattle. Mr. Schoch was a picture of robust health, so that the news came as a distinct shock to his hosts of friends and business associates.

Wednesday he went with W.R. Conner and George Newell to Sand Point as the guests of H.O. Williams, a Seattle insurance man. On the fifteenth hole Mr. Schoch made a "birdie" three and walked over to the tee of the sixteenth hole. He passed a casual remark to his companions about his score on the last hole and slumped over on the bench—dead. Heart failure is believed to have been the cause of death. He was 51 years old.

Mr. Schoch had ever been interested and active in sports, and in his younger days, both in his native state of Iowa and in Everett, he was a star in baseball. At one time he pitched for the Seattle team of the Coast League. At another time he pitched the Everett team to 27 straight victories.

Mr. Schoch was manager for the Northwestern Mutual Life Insurance Company for the district that embraced Snohomish and adjacent counties. He was also a director of the Security National Bank. He was formerly president of the Port of Everett and was prominent in Masonic activities. Mr. Schoch was also active in the Chamber of Commerce, the Rotary Club, the Everett Country Club, the Cascade Club, and as a member of the Everett park board was active in the work of that body.

He is survived by a widow, Mrs. Kathryn Schoch, three daughters, Miss Mildred, Miss Marian, and Miss Kathryn, and a son, Clifton.

Funeral services will be held at 1:30 o'clock Monday afternoon at the Elks Lodge.

Heinie Heitmuller (1883-1912)

One of the stars of the championship Everett team in 1905 was Heinie Heitmuller, an outstanding athlete from the University of California. He played in the outfield for Everett, and is credited by the Encyclopedia of Minor League Baseball with winning the league batting title. In 1906 Heinie moved up to the Pacific Coast League, and in 1909 and 1910 played with the Philadelphia Athletics in the American League. By 1912 he was back in the Pacific Coast League with the Los Angeles Angels. Throughout the season he was in the thick of the race for the league batting title. On September 28th, Los Angeles played a double header in which Heinie got two doubles and four singles to raise his average to .335. Tragically, the next day Heinie Heitmuller was struck down by typhoid fever. He declined rapidly and died just nine days later. He was 29 years old. But that's not the end of Heinie's baseball story. At the time he died, his batting average was second in the league. The leader, however, went into a hitting slump, so at the end of the season, Heinie had the highest average. He will be forever remembered in baseball history as the Dead Man who won the 1912 Pacific Coast League batting championship.

AFTERWORD

Baseball was my first love—before I discovered girls. As a boy I lived in Seattle listening to Leo Lassen, "The Voice of Summer," broadcast the games of the Seattle Rainiers. Leo's skill at recreating games from the teletype was uncanny; I was an adult before I could accept the fact that he did not actually attend the out-of-town games (if there was a break in the transmission Leo would call a rain delay). Leo instilled a life-long love of baseball in a generation of Pacific Northwest kids.

We did not just listen to baseball, we played it—when it wasn't raining too hard. Playing in the fog was fun. We may have daydreamed about playing professional baseball, but reality in the form of military service wiped out that prospect for most of us. Besides, there was very little money in baseball at that time, and playing for glory was no longer appealing.

When I got out of the Marines after the Korean Conflict I attended the University of Washington on the GI Bill and majored in accounting. After twenty years as a CPA I went into the timber business, but my years as an auditor gave me a nose for obscure facts which I have put to good use in doing historical research. It's not that I enjoy digging in musty-dusty archives, but at least I'm willing to do it.

I am now retired from business and live with my wife and dog on Fidalgo Island near Anacortes, Washington. I spend much of my time researching and writing about early baseball in the Northwest. My wife says I am in my second childhood.

Dave Larson, member, Society for American Baseball Research
March, 2006 (davbev@fidalgo.net)

Photo Credits

Page